Success

INTERNATIONAL

REVISED EDITION
ENGLISH SKILLS FOR IGCSE

Workbook

Endorsed by
University of Cambridge International Examinations

Marian Barry

GEORGIAN PRESS

Georgian Press (Jersey) Limited
Pirouet House
Union Street
St Helier
Jersey JE4 8QZ
Channel Islands

www.georgianpress.co.uk

First published by Georgian Press (Jersey) Limited 2001
This revised edition first published 2005
Reprinted 2006

ISBN 1-873630-46-8

Produced by AMR Limited

Illustrations by Art Construction

Printed in Egypt by International Printing House

Contents

Introduction

This Workbook is designed to be used in conjunction with the Revised Edition of *Success International* coursebook and, for the convenience of those using the course, many exercises are cross-referenced to coursebook pages. However, the Workbook can also be used successfully without reference to the course, as the exercises are self-explanatory and complete in themselves. The answers are provided in *Success International Teacher's Book*.

Any student preparing for the Cambridge IGCSE in E2L examination will benefit from this book, as, indeed, will students at intermediate to upper-intermediate level generally, who wish to broaden and consolidate their language ability in English.

Aims and objectives

The Workbook aims to consolidate and test students' understanding of the language and themes introduced in *Success International*.

For example, Unit 3 of the course focuses on note-taking and summary-writing, and the main topic is the importance of sport, fitness and diet in our lives. The Workbook unit follows this up with detailed practice on points of vocabulary, writing more concisely, note-taking, and summarising a 'mini' text.

Similarly, Unit 8 teaches story-telling skills, so the corresponding Workbook unit provides a wide variety of exercises to further develop narrative technique.

Flexibility of use

SELF-ACCESS

Students can use the Workbook without help from the teacher, making it very suitable for homework and private study.

IN THE CLASSROOM

The Workbook can be used during lessons to complement the work being done with the coursebook.

TESTS

Exercises from the Workbook can be set as periodic language tests during the term, to check assimilation of coursebook material.

How students will benefit

Students are given substantial additional practice in the language, in exercise formats which provide a useful contrast to those in *Success International* coursebook, and different kinds of challenges.

The Workbook supports exam achievement by showing students good and less good examples of language. Text completion exercises, when finished, provide valuable model answers to typical exam questions, highlighting the importance of a mature writing style, with appropriate tone and register and audience awareness.

The aim of *Success International* is to increase student independence by encouraging a mature attitude to learning and an understanding of meaning. The Workbook complements this by encouraging students to work out answers for themselves, to take care in checking their work, and to make sure their answers make complete sense. This will help students mature educationally, and will reduce an over-reliance on the teacher.

Range of exercises

The following list is not exhaustive but gives a flavour of the range of exercises in the Workbook. Students are offered plenty of variety, to keep them interested and on their toes.

- vocabulary development, idioms, phrasal verbs
- prefixes and suffixes
- collocation
- spelling and punctuation
- use of prepositions
- sentence construction
- grammar revision
- textual organisation, logical reasoning and understanding meaning
- paragraphing
- tone and register
- developing a mature writing style
- understanding visual information (maps, graphs, charts, etc)

UNIT 1 — Happiness and Success

1 Quick language check ▶

Choose the correct word or phrase from each pair in italics.

1 George ran his own business *during/for* a year.

2 The illness made me *realise/to realise* how important good health is.

3 If *I pass/I'll pass* the test, I'll get a present from my parents.

4 You must *pay/to pay* for things before taking them out of the shop.

5 You should *eating/eat* more fruit and vegetables.

6 I *am/have* already finished the book you lent me.

7 This medicine might not help your cold but it will *make/do* you no harm.

8 We got off the bus and continued our journey *by/on* foot.

9 Lizzie told me why *she was/was she* feeling miserable.

2 Formal and informal styles ▶   SB p10

Replace each informal word or phrase in italics with a more formal one. Choose from the words in the box.

> expensive   newspaper   dismissed   enthusiastic about
> bored or unhappy   children   prefer   glasses

1 They took the *kids* to an adventure playground.

2 He was *sacked* for constantly taking time off work.

3 If I feel *fed up*, I go for a long walk across the hills.

4 Mona's *into* pop music but I *go for* classical.

5 Sam made a lot of money by selling computers and moved to a *posh* area of town.

6 Have you got today's *paper*?

7 Has anyone seen my *specs*?

3 Adjective suffixes: *-ful* and *-less* ▶

Complete each sentence by choosing a word from the box and adding *-ful* or *-less* to make an adjective. The first one has been done for you.

> speech   motion   colour   harm   friend   help
> point   heart   thank   thought

1 A newborn baby is completely *helpless*   .

2 Gregory chose a bright, _____ wallpaper for his bedroom.

3 It was _____ trying to find our way in a strange town without a map.

4 It was _____ of her to send me flowers when I was ill.

5   Bill has no feeling for anyone; people say he is _____ .

6   People sometimes say they feel lonely, but being completely _____ is
    very rare.

7   When I was told I had won the lottery, I was _____ with delight.

8   Adult medicine can be _____ to children.

9   Let's be _____ for the good things in our lives.

10 The small sailboat was _____ on the calm sea.

4 Job suffixes: -ant, -er, -ist, -or ▶   SB p12

**Make each word in brackets into a noun to fill the gap, by adding the correct suffix.
Be careful – you may need to make spelling changes too.**

1   Luke is a _____ in a pop group and his brother is a _____ .
    (drum, football)

2   My aunt is a _____ of a multinational company. (direct)

3   I'd like to speak to the project _____ , please. (supervise)

4   Miguel used to work as a _____ and _____ . (paint, decorate)

5   I'd love to be an _____ in a television studio. (assist)

6   Angela is training to become a _____ helping people with relationship
    difficulties. (psychology)

7   He has a highpowered job as an _____ . It wouldn't appeal to me. (account)

8   Hussein is an _____ and is very interested in ways to protect the
    environment. (ecology)

9   I asked the telephone _____ to check the number for me. (operate)

10 Her job as a _____ involves translating instruction booklets from English
    into other languages. (translate)

5 Text completion ▶

**Read this text about the search for happiness and choose a word from the box to fill each
space. You will need to change the form of some of the verbs.**

Adjectives	*Nouns*	*Verbs*	
happier	loneliness	afford	predict
miserable	pressure	believe	replace
vital	wealth	blame	
	youth		

The search for happiness

Everyone wants to be happy, but people rarely agree on what happiness is or what the

(1) _____ ingredients for happiness are. Money certainly seems to play a part,

and studies have shown that people on low incomes struggling to (2) _____

basic things like food and housing are less happy than those who are comfortably off.

However, once an adequate income has been achieved, increasing (3) _____

does not seem to make us more content. The super rich are no more satisfied with life than those on a modest income.

People in their twenties and fifties are said to be (4) _____ than those in their thirties and forties, perhaps because the latter two groups are under the most (5) _____ to build careers and bring up families. If (6) _____ and a high income are not crucial to happiness, then what is essential? Ancient philosophers (7) _____ that freedom, thought and friendship were the key elements.

It is impossible to say whether people were more (8) _____ centuries ago than they are today. Despite rising levels of affluence, however, the World Health Organisation (9) _____ that the second biggest illness in the developed world this century will be depression. Psychologists (10) _____ the problems of community breakdown, (11) _____ and isolation on the stresses of modern life and the way technology is (12) _____ human contact.

6 Figurative language ▶   SB p13

Replace the figurative language in italics with expressions from the box.

very sad	very noisy	very proud	disappeared	very soft
	reminders	based on	complex trap	

1 Danielle was *bursting with pride* when she talked about the prize she had won.

2 We got a *heart-rending* letter giving an account of my grandmother's illness.

3 My beliefs about life after death are not *rooted in* any particular philosophy.

4 Her anger *melted away* when she saw how sorry the little boy was.

5 There were *echoes* of her own childhood in the novel she wrote about a poor family who emigrated to the United States.

6 He didn't realise that telling the first lie would create a *tangled web* of deceit.

7 Lovingly, she stroked the baby's *velvety* skin.

8 There was a *howling* wind all night.

7 Homophones ▶   SB pp13–14

Choose the correct word from each pair in italics.

1 Did you *worn/warn* her about the storm that is forecast for tonight?

2 My grandfather *fought/fort* in the Second World *Wore/War*.

3 Matthew *ate/eight* all the food in the fridge.

4 The curtains I bought in the sale were reduced because there was a *floor/flaw* in the material.

5 *Wrote/rote* learning is a good way to remember arithmetic tables.

6 'Haven't you *groan/grown*!' said grandma when the children came to visit.

7 Magda is extremely *frank/franc* and will always give her truthful opinion.

8 The wedding cake had three *tiers/tears*.

Choose three of the words which you crossed out and use them in sentences of your own.

1 _____

2 _____

3 _____

8 Text completion ▶   SB p14

Read this text about Albert Einstein and choose the correct word from each pair in italics.

A great thinker

Scientists used to think that matter could not be created nor destroyed. They also believed that the same principles applied to energy. However, in the first few years of the twentieth century, the German scientist Albert Einstein came *out/up* with a different idea. He predicted that it should be possible to change mass into energy. Einstein's idea – his Theory of Relativity – was first proved *by/in* 1932. Einstein showed that a small amount of matter could be changed into a vast amount of energy. This made the development of nuclear energy *happen/possible*.

Born in 1879, Einstein was an unusual child who did not speak until he was three years old. Early photographs show a serious and intense-looking little boy. When he was twelve, he *learned/taught* himself Euclidean geometry. He hated school, however, and at the age of fifteen he used the fact that the family had moved house as an *excuse/explain* for not going to school for a year. He finally graduated in 1900 by studying the lecture notes of a classmate.

Einstein grew into a brilliant and *imaginative/imagining* young man who was *passionately/perfectly* interested in science. He was also a very lively correspondent and *did/made* a point of replying to any letters he received from children. His intelligent, amiable looking face with its untidy mop of silvery hair is well known, *apart/yet* as a young man he had short, coal-black hair and a serious, thoughtful appearance. The face of the Jedi Master Yoda in the Star Wars films was *copied/inspired* by Einstein's wise expression.

Sadly, Einstein's theories were used to develop nuclear weapons and ultimately the atomic bomb which was dropped on Japan during the Second World War. Einstein never *forgave/upset* himself for the uses to which his discoveries were put. Shortly before he died in 1955, he wrote a letter to the newspapers urging scientists to unite to *end/prevent* the possibility of another nuclear war in the future.

9 Comparing information in charts ▶

Study the bar chart showing the connection between literacy and happiness in Britain. Then answer the questions below.

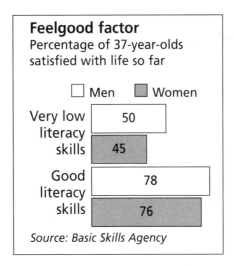

Feelgood factor
Percentage of 37-year-olds satisfied with life so far

☐ Men   ▨ Women

Very low literacy skills: 50 / 45
Good literacy skills: 78 / 76

Source: Basic Skills Agency

True or false?

1 Less than half the women who had low literacy skills were happy with their lives.

2 Men, overall, were more satisfied with their lives than women.

3 More than three-quarters of men and women who had a good standard of literacy said they were happy with their lives.

10 Sentence correction ▶

In each of the following sentences a word has been left out. Read the sentence carefully and add the missing word in the right place. The first one has been done for you.

1 I went ∧ bed early last night because I was tired.
       to

2 The doctor told Monika to give smoking.

3 I listened to a programme about happiness the radio.

4 What time you finish work this evening?

5 When all the work been done, we went to see a film.

6 She was very surprised when Yannis asked her marry him.

7 England is not big as Spain.

8 The school breaks for the holidays next Thursday.

9 I have appointment with the doctor at eleven tomorrow morning.

10 The kitchen smells of fresh bread because I been baking all morning.

11 Apostrophes: Omission of letters ▶   SB p15

Add apostrophes in these sentences where necessary.

1 I havent decided what to wear to the party yet.

2 I wish youd be more careful. Youre always breaking things.

3 Shes got a son, Rory, whos nine.

4 Dont you think youd better wear a coat as its raining?

5 Lets meet soon for a drink. Its ages since Ive seen you.

6 He doesnt know where theyve gone, does he?

7 Arent you hot in that thick sweater?

8 This coffees lost its flavour.

12 How important is literacy? ▶   SB pp18–19

A student wrote this letter to the newspaper about improving literacy standards in her country. Build up a complete letter from the prompts.

Dear Editor,

Literacy be/very important/people's happiness/and development/country. Studies show/people/unable/read or write/more likely/be dissatisfied/their lives. They lack confidence/find/difficult/get/job. In addition/they not help/their children/schoolwork/or play active part/their community. They find/difficult/do ordinary things/like read newspapers/fill in forms. Some/feel ashamed. They cover up/problems/and pretend/can read.

I think/it be very important/that people/can't read or write/get help. In our area/there be/literacy scheme/help adults/improve/skills in reading and writing. Schemes like this/help/government/achieve goal/100% literacy/our country.

Yours faithfully,
Vicki Sansa

13 *Would* and *used to* ▶   SB p18

Would is similar to *used to*. Both can refer to repeated past actions, but only *used to* can refer to past states. Example: *He used to own a shop in the town centre.* (NOT *would*)

Read these pairs of sentences about the past. If one is incorrect, cross it out.

1 I used to get up early and feed the hens/I would get up early and feed the hens.

2 He used to have a dog called Sophie/He would have a dog called Sophie.

3 I used to visit my grandma on Sunday/I would visit my grandma on Sunday.

4 They used to live in a beautiful villa/They would live in a beautiful villa.

5 Dena used to have black curly hair/Dena would have black curly hair.

6 Mario used to be my best friend/Mario would be my best friend.

Now write a few sentences about your childhood activities using *would*.

1 _____

2 _____

3 _____

14 Describing character ▶   SB p20

Match each description of a person's character with a word from the box. There is one word you don't need.

> sensitive   good-natured   placid   secretive   ambitious
> untidy   absent-minded   optimistic   artistic

1 My father tends to forget ordinary everyday things and often goes to work without his wallet or briefcase.

2 She gets on well with people and will offer to help you if you need it.

3 I don't like sitting next to Joanna. She leaves apple cores, sweet wrappers and old tissues all over her desk.

4 Javier is very keen to have a successful career and regularly changes his job to improve his prospects.

5 Their new baby is only two months old but he hardly cries at all.

6 The new manager is a very positive thinker and believes in a good future.

7 Melanie paints lovely pictures and has decorated her home beautifully.

8 She doesn't share her ideas or plans with anyone.

15 Vocabulary check ▶   SB p20

Decide whether or not the following sentences make proper sense. Give each one either a ✔ or a ✗. Think carefully about the words in italics.

1 Ali's *close-cropped* hair reached almost to his shoulders.

2 The radio presenter's *grating* voice was pleasant to listen to.

3 *Bushy* eyebrows can also be described as fine.

4 A *genial* person is easy to talk to.

5 His *rugged* appearance suggested he spent a lot of time working outdoors.

6 A *retired* person no longer works for a living.

7 Tara took a lot of care over her clothes and make-up and always looked *scruffy*.

8 The doctor told Paul he was too *skinny* and should try to put on weight.

9 The actress was proud of her long, thick, *luxuriant* hair.

10 I was afraid to tell the new doctor my problems because he was so *severe-looking*.

11 Mr Wei needed someone strong to work in his restaurant and turned down most applicants because of their *robust* appearance.

12 Donna could hardly see because her *fringe* was so long.

13 The *clean-shaven* man had a black beard and moustache.

14 Lorraine's *toddler* enjoys running and cycling.

16 Negative prefixes ▶ SB p20

Make these twenty words into their opposites by writing them after the correct prefix below. You may need to use your dictionary.

| patient happy legal understand tidy secure responsible |
| literate prepared correct regular appear lock enthusiastic |
| conscious significant sympathetic obey behave possible |

un _____

il _____

im _____

in _____

ir _____

dis _____

mis _____

Now choose four of the words you have made and put them in sentences of your own.

1 _____

2 _____

3 _____

4 _____

17 Writing in a more mature style ▶ SB pp22–23

Try to rewrite this description in a more mature style.

This is my grandmother. She is old. She is small. She has got fair skin. She has got brown eyes. She has white hair. She has a nice personality. She has got a bad leg. She smiles a lot but she has pains in her knee. She has arthritis. She paints pictures of things like birds, animals and flowers. She remembers my birthday. She buys me nice presents. She wears a gold locket around her neck. It is from my grandfather. He bought it for her when they got married. She likes it very much.

18 Sentence correction ▶

In each of these sentences there is one extra word which shouldn't be there. Find it and cross it out.

1 John was thoughtful and good-natured him and popular with everyone.

2 I suggest you to keep a vocabulary notebook for new words.

3 My hair it needs cutting soon.

4 He would prefers coffee without sugar.

5 Al failed his driving test, not because of his bad driving, but because of his eyesight was poor.

6 If you're hoping to go in to college next term, you should apply now.

7 It's a well-organised school, where the pupils they are very happy.

8 I would have been able to do such more studying for the exams if I hadn't had to help at home.

9 Although his clothes were not new, but he looked neat and smart.

10 It was there a beautiful place to live.

19 Text correction ▶

In this article for a teenage magazine, there is one mistake in each complete sentence. Try to find the mistakes and correct them.

Someone I admire

One of my favourite writers are Charlotte Brontë. She is born in the early nineteenth century when women had far fewer opportunities than they have now. She lived in a small village in Yorkshire and she took great pleasure in walked on the moors near her home.

From a young age, Charlotte was determined to become a writer and she begin writing stories when she was still very young. Many of the personal sufferings and hardships she experienced as a child she later put on her books. One of the saddest things that happened to her was being sent away to a boarding school when she was treated very harshly. She believed the cruel school regime was responsible to the death of her dear sister, Maria.

In her personal life, Charlotte were very caring and compassionate. She look after her brother and her father when they were both very ill, despite being in poor health herself. She also gave support to her other two sisters Emily and Anne, which were also very talented. They were struggling to expressing themselves as writers too.

Charlotte's more famous novel is *Jane Eyre*. It was an instant success and is still read all over the world, perhaps because its themes of love and the fight for justice are universal? Like Charlotte, Jane Eyre was small, slight and delicate-looked. Like Charlotte, she was also forced to earn her own living as governess.

Sadly, Charlotte died just months later she got married at the age of 38. It's so sad to think she died just as she had found emotional fulfilment and when her creative powers were at they're height.

1   Open and closed questions ▶   SB pp25–26

Closed questions usually require *yes/no* answers. Open questions invite a more complete answer. Notice that questions beginning *Tell me* . . . don't need a question mark.

Mark the following questions 'open' or 'closed'. The first pair has been done for you.

1   **a**   Do you get on well with your brother?   *closed*

    b   Tell me about your relationship with your brother.   *open*

2   **a**   What's the area you live in like?

    b   Is this a good area to live in?

3   **a**   How do you celebrate your birthday?

    b   Do you celebrate your birthday in any way?

4   **a**   Is your house nice?

    b   What do you most enjoy about the house you live in?

5   **a**   Are your neighbours nice?

    b   Tell me more about your neighbours.

2   Forming open questions ▶   SB pp25–26

Rewrite these closed questions to make them open.

1   Have you lived in your neighbourhood a long time?

_____

2   Have there been any changes?

_____

3   Do you like growing up there?

_____

4   Do you have nice friends?

_____

5   Do you belong to a club?

_____

6   Are there places to spend free time near you?

_____

3   Vocabulary check ▶   SB pp27–28

Choose the correct word from each pair in italics.

1   The school does not allow any kind of bullying, *name-calling/name-dropping* or other kinds of abuse.

2   She is not *academic/single-minded* and prefers sport to studying science and maths.

3   Although their father is a famous actor, the family are quite *downtrodden/down-to-earth* and the children have to help at home and save up for things they want.

4 The family are quite *go-ahead/go for it* and want to try new things. For example, there was no social club around here so they started one.

5 Our village is a very *close-up/close-knit* community. If there is a problem, everyone helps.

6 Fabrice took his toy engine apart because he was *curious/naive* about the way it worked.

7 The company is *contemplating/conspiring* setting up a new office in Melbourne.

8 Although Mrs Stavrou is rich, she never gives her dog enough to eat. I hate seeing such *blatant/inadvertent* ill-treatment of an animal.

9 We *relish/relic* the idea of taking part in an exchange scheme – we'll make new friends and visit exciting places.

10 Youssef was determined to train as a fitness instructor and never let his asthma *hold his head up/hold him back*.

4 Text correction ▶   SB pp29–30

Read this description of a special place. In all the sentences *except one*, there is an extra word which shouldn't be there. Find these words and cross them out. There are 13 to find.

A special memory by Outa Seppa

A place that holds a special memory for me is at the decorative iron bridge right in the centre of our town. The bridge itself is quite modern but it has been built with care and of skill. I think it will last long for generations.

When I was younger, I used to meet there my best friend Maya on the bridge after school. We'd laugh and chat us and throw bread to the graceful white swans swimming soundlessly on the water below. From the bridge we could see more into the market. We'd watch the hustle and bustle of the crowds weaving their way through the colourful stalls and catch up fragrant whiffs of cooking from the open-air café.

High on the bridge, however, the atmosphere well was peaceful and tranquil. The sun glinted on the water and we could do relax and unwind in its warmth while we talked about our plans.

The bridge will always be a beautiful but now it has a sad memory for me. One day Maya told me the sad news that she would be moving over to another country with her family. I was devastated. Maya and I wrote letters at first but somehow we got us out of touch. Whenever I pass to the bridge I look up and wonder what Maya is doing now.

5 Language to describe places ▶   SB p30

Read each short text and choose the best way of completing it.

1   My favourite place is definitely the flower shop. Just walking into that _____ environment and smelling the exotic blooms lifts my spirits.

    a cosy   **c** muted
    b fragrant   **d** vibrant

2   The best view around is from the top of Highfields Hill. On a clear day you can see for miles. After a day of urban stress, it gives me a whole new perspective on my problems. It's a strenuous climb but definitely _____ .

    a isolated   **c** off the beaten track
    b worth the effort   **d** only five minutes away

3   Have you ever visited the ruined castle at midnight? There's not a sound, the moon throws great shadows over the stones and it's easy to imagine the kings and queens who lived there long ago. The atmosphere is rather _____ but, even though I feel a bit scared, I like to linger there.

    a civilised   **c** eerie
    b dimly-lit   **d** invigorating

4   Where I live, we have glorious sunsets. When I've got time, I love to go outside and watch the sky turn red and yellow and finally go completely dark. Even though I live on a noisy city street, the sunsets allow me to _____ .

    a feel secure   **c** experience the beauty of nature
    b enjoy my own company **d** marvel at the wonderful things
                                          people have created

5   If you're free this weekend, why not take a bus out of town and visit the country park at Comens? You can walk through our flower-studded woods, catching glimpses of the wildlife, or enjoy a relaxing picnic by the lake. The whole family will find

    _____ .

    a it has a light-hearted, bustling   **c** it makes a great change from
        atmosphere   life in the city
    b it warm and cosy   **d** they see it through new eyes

6   I'm lucky where I live because there are plenty of open spaces, and I have friends living nearby. Having a game of football in the park with a group of friends is a great way to _____ after a tough day at school.

    a appreciate the special atmosphere   **c** feel exhilarated
    b relax and unwind   **d** be uplifted

6 Word formation ▶

Read this article a student wrote for a magazine. To fill each gap, choose a word from the box and change it into the correct form. The first one has been done for you.

inspiration lightly convert reduce
swim charming relaxation tradition owner

A breath of fresh air

My town has lots going for it – parks, a (1) *swimming* pool and several museums. One place, however, has become a definite favourite of mine. Recently, a shop and café, Trade Winds, has opened in a (2) _____ warehouse only five minutes away from the centre of town.

The people who (3) _____ the shop used to live in Africa and they import things from all over that continent. You can buy (4) _____ handmade jewellery, paintings, gifts and pottery. You can browse for as long as you want. It's the kind of place where no-one minds how long you stay or forces you to buy anything. Every now and then there is a half-price sale with genuine (5) _____ , which is a bonus if you are on a tight budget.

Trade Winds has a wonderful, (6) _____ atmosphere and upstairs the café is warm and friendly too. I often visit the shop at weekends and meet my friends in the café for some hot chocolate or a (7) _____ snack. We can laugh and talk and forget our everyday problems for a while. Trade Winds has brought new life into the community. Our town still retains an old world (8) _____ , but new people and new ideas keep it an appealing and (9) _____ place to live.

7 Using adjectives ▶   SB p30

The adjectives in italics in these sentences have all been mixed up! Can you change them back to their correct positions?

1   I love the *breathtaking* atmosphere of Tigona, the *luxurious*, unspoilt fishing village where we spent our summer holidays.

2   From our balcony, we have a *shady* view of the mountains.

3   Our town has a *fragrant* archaeological zone which attracts many visitors.

4   My aunt and uncle have an extremely stylish city apartment with *sleepy* rooms and *picturesque* furniture.

5   I love nothing better on a hot afternoon than lying in a *spacious* spot in the garden, drinking in the *fascinating* scent of the flowers and listening to the lazy hum of the insects.

8 Developing a more mature style ▶

Try to rewrite this description in a more interesting way, using a more mature style.

I have my own bedroom. There is a window in the bedroom. From the window you can see the garden. There is a walnut tree in the garden. The tree is close to my window. I can pick nuts from the tree. My favourite thing in my bedroom is my bed. It is comfortable. It is soft. It has many cushions. There is a bedspread. The bedspread is nice. It is from India. It is silk. The colours of the bedspread are very nice. They are not bright. They are kind of dull colours. I read on my bed. I dream on my bed. My bedroom has a good atmosphere.

9 Choose the best word ▶   SB p31

Choose the correct word to complete each sentence.

1 People often prefer living in new houses as the _____ costs are usually lower than in old buildings.

   a support   **b** maintenance   **c** repairing   **d** developing

2 Long-distance buses may have toilet _____ on them.

   a equipment   **b** resources   **c** facilities   **d** rooms

3 We worked out a(n) _____ for our holiday so we knew how much we could afford to spend each day.

   a budget   **b** allowance   **c** account   **d** savings

4 The bookshop on the High Street has closed down and the _____ is/are up for sale.

   a commerce   **b** premises   **c** belongings   **d** trade

5 The children were completely _____ and refused to do what the teacher told them.

   a disorganised   **b** displeased   **c** undisciplined   **d** unpleasant

6 The manager plans to _____ the project after six months to see if the money being spent on it is worthwhile.

   a respond   **b** review   **c** recall   **d** report

7 A _____ restaurant like the Delhi Brasserie deserves to be successful.

   a well-fed   **b** well-run   **c** well-balanced   **d** well-made

8 We didn't think it was right to build a supermarket in the middle of a quiet _____ street.

   a residential   **b** regional   **c** community   **d** urban

9 I would have liked a white sofa and white armchairs for the living room, but as our children are very small, we decided the idea was _____ .

   a imperfect   **b** impersonal   **c** impossible   **d** impractical.

10 Everdale United supporters became very _____ when their team won the match.

   a rowdy   **b** disturbing   **c** loudly   **d** racket

10 Text completion ▶

SB p33

Read this factual information about fostering children and choose the correct word from each pair in italics.

Living with a foster family

Children are usually cared for in their own families, until they are old enough to live independently. Sometimes, *however/nevertheless*, parents or relatives are not able to look after their children. In this case, the state will often take responsibility *for/of* them. The children may be looked after in children's homes, or fostering or adoption is *arranged/ordered* with families. Fostering means taking a child into your family for a *duration/period* of time and caring for him or her as your own child. The government makes *earnings/payments* to the family to cover extra food, clothes and other necessities while the child is staying there.

Fostering allows children to experience normal family life. Foster families are very carefully *selected/singled* to ensure that the child will *adapt/change* happily. Foster parents are often *apprehensive/upset* at first, but most placements are successful. A fostering *link/liaison* officer helps place children in suitable families. He or she stays in contact to make sure everyone is *coping/surviving* well with the situation. Children who need the company of brothers and sisters will be placed with large families, *also/whereas* a child who requires a lot of individual attention will usually be placed in a small family. The foster child may make lifelong friendships with the foster family and continue to keep in *company/touch* long after he or she has grown up.

11 Sentence correction ▶

Add the missing word in the right place in each of these sentences.

1   We're going buy a new fridge this weekend.
2   Your cousin can stay with us as long he wants to.
3   Katerina made us a lovely lunch green vegetables and chicken.
4   I'm tired, so I think I go to bed early tonight.
5   William is old enough to walk to school on own.
6   If you don't bring your swimming things, you won't able to go swimming.
7   There's always the chance meeting someone you know at the market.
8   If we known you were in town, we would have invited you to dinner.
9   How long you been saving up for a new bicycle?
10   It snowing hard when they left for the airport.

12 Understanding information in a table ▶

Study this table which gives information about families wanting to foster a child. Then choose the best family for each child described below.

Family name	Period of time able to foster	Type of area	Will child share a bedroom?	Age of youngest in family	Pets	Family's leisure activities
Carter	Short-term	Town – suburbs	✗	Toddler 2 years	Dog	Photography
Khan	Indefinite	Large city	✔	Baby 6 months	Kitten	Bowling, swimming
Sanchez	Short-term	Centre of medium-sized town	✔	Twins 18 years	New puppy	Cycling, fishing
Bloome	Indefinite	Small village	✗	No children	Dog	Football, basketball
Morel	Long-term	Large village	✔	Boy 4 years	Hamster, rabbit	Cinema, reading
Walsh	Short-term	Remote rural area	✗	Boy 16 years, Girl 14 years	Horse, guinea pig, budgie	Horse-riding
Lilkova	Long-term	Large village	✔	Girl 11 years	None	Bird-watching

Write the name of the family you would choose for each child.

1   A girl of 16 who would like to live in a town and be the youngest in the family.
_____

2   A boy who prefers indoor activities and requires fostering for a considerable length of time. _____

3   A boy who doesn't want to share parental attention with other children.
_____

4   A girl who would prefer an urban environment and is allergic to dogs.
_____

5   A 15-year-old boy who wants to live with teenagers about his own age and would like the chance to get involved in caring for a pet. _____

6   A teenage boy who would prefer a bedroom of his own and would like a younger foster brother or sister. _____

7   A nine-year-old girl who likes the countryside but does not want to live in an isolated environment. _____

13 Text completion ▶   SB p36

Read this text about the way new words have come into English and think of ONE suitable word to fill each gap.

English – an ever-changing language

Linguists believe the vocabulary of English consists (1) _____ more than 500,000 words. About half of them are thought to come (2) _____ other languages. (3) _____ example, over 1,000 years ago Viking invaders arriving from Denmark and Norway brought the words *husband, sky, take* and *leg*. The (4) _____ *they, them* and *their* are also Scandinavian. Cultural and political association with France has led (5) _____ the adoption of many French words into English, (6) _____ as *naive, genre, liaison* and *chef*.

England and Scotland (7) _____ many battles in the past and the word *slogan* was a Scottish war cry. Contact (8) _____ countries outside Europe resulted in *potato* from Haiti, *tomato* and *chocolate* from Mexico, *tea* and *ketchup* from China, and *kebab* and *zero* from (9) _____ Middle East.

Settlers in North America invented words (10) _____ describe things (11) _____ were seeing for the first time, which is how we got *grasshopper* and *rattlesnake*. The expression *OK* originated in America, although the experts are not (12) _____ how or why it was created. *Boomerang* is (13) _____ native Australian word adopted into English (14) _____ early explorers of Australia.

Language changes (15) _____ small ways all the time, and it is particularly noticeable when new things or ideas (16) _____ created, which (17) _____ how we come to have *teenager, babysitter* and *mouse mat*, and are able (18) _____ talk about *surfing the net*.

14 Idioms round-up ▶

Choose the best definition for each of the idiomatic expressions in italics.

1   They are a family who always *stick together*.

   a   support and help each other   **c**   hardly see each other
   b   are afraid to leave each other   **d**   give each other money

2   When my father lost his job, *things were a bit tight*.

   a   we couldn't afford new clothes   **c**   our financial situation was difficult
   b   he was very angry   **d**   there was a bad atmosphere at home

3   With Mia's fantastic qualifications, *the sky's the limit*.

   a   she expects achievement without working for it   **c**   there's no limit to what she will be able to do
   b   she could work for an airline   **d**   she already has a better career than other people

4   Before Anil came to live with us, he had *been through a lot*.

   a   lived with many different families   c   travelled in several countries
   b   suffered some bad experiences   d   spent too much money

5   Buying extra medicine for the baby's illness *was a drain on their resources*.

   a   used up their money   c   made them borrow money
   b   was an unnecessary expense   d   increased their budget

6   Tony wants to leave school without taking any exams but his parents have *dug their heels in* over it.

   a   talked to the teachers   c   had terrible arguments
   b   suggested he wait   d   refused to change their mind

15 Correcting a letter ▶   SB p38

This letter is about an exchange visit which will have to be postponed. Put in the punctuation and paragraphing. Don't forget to read it first to get the sense.

dear isabel

it was lovely to hear from you and I apologise for not getting in touch sooner
unfortunately weve had some family problems dad has had a pain in his back for quite a
long time and the doctor has just told him hes going to need an operation hell have to stay
in hospital for a while and when he comes out hell need a complete rest im awfully sorry
to disappoint you but I think we had better postpone your holiday with us until dad is
better mum and I will have to go to the hospital every day and it wouldnt be much fun for
you to be left at home alone also the trips we had hoped to do would have to be
cancelled as neither dad or mum will be able to drive us anywhere I am so sorry again to
disappoint you I was really looking forward to your coming over everyone hopes you will
be able to come next summer and then we really will have a great time
all the best

kelly

16 Improving the tone of a letter ▶   SB p39

Try to rewrite this letter to an exchange visitor in a more welcoming tone and a mature style. Use a suitable opening and closing sentence too.

Dear Ahmed,

I've got a younger brother called Joseph. He is very annoying. He is only nice if you
do something he wants. You are going to come to school with me too. I don't think
you will learn much. Don't sit with Tom, Ben or Dave because they are a pain. You
can sit with me. Our form teacher is Mrs Johnson. If you forget your spelling book
(Thursday) or sports kit (Mon and Wed) she can be very touchy. She can be nice.
The other teachers are angry if they are not being kind. We will go out after school.
If you are homesick, you can go back home.

Love,

Oliver

UNIT 3 — Sport and Fitness

1 Is sport always fun? ▶   SB p44

Read each short text and choose the best way of completing it.

1 Paco was delighted to be chosen as the captain of the football team. Now he can
_____ .

    a stand around on the football field   **c** pick players for the team
    b approach the sport safely   **d** wait to be selected

2 Some people say sport at school is unfair and should be banned. Others, however, feel
it is a chance to enjoy _____ , as it helps children learn about both
losing and winning.

    a traditional sports   **c** a relaxing experience
    b healthy competition   **d** up-to-date activities

3 When Miriam was small, although she tried hard, she couldn't play ball games. She had
difficulty listening properly when the teacher spoke to her. Her school arranged a
special programme which has really helped _____ . Now she can listen
for much longer, and she's learned to play tennis.

    a her enjoy being outside in all weathers   **c** her self-discipline
    b her think positively   **d** her concentration and co-ordination

4 I dislike sports where you have to keep up with the team. I prefer activities like yoga
or jogging, because they have no pressure and allow you to _____ .

    a develop self-confidence   **c** work at your own pace
    b appreciate fair play   **d** become more competitive

2 Linking ideas ▶   SB p45

Match the halves to make complete sentences.

1 Hassan is a very competitive child and always …

2 For children who aren't good at sport, sports day …

3 People say that losing at sport isn't bad for children. On the contrary, they …

4 It was raining so heavily yesterday that we …

5 It was a very close match and our team …

6 I found the pictures of starving children on the TV news …

7 The girl who broke her leg playing basketball …

a most distressing.

b has to have the highest marks in class.

c can be an annual torment.

d won by a single goal we scored just before the end.

e abandoned the idea of swimming in the open-air pool.

f believe it is character building.

g is being comforted by her mother.

3 Making comparisons ▶ SB p45

'For the children who can fly like the wind, sports day is no problem.'
Complete each of the following comparisons with a noun from the box. There is one more noun than you need.

a horse   a fish   a log   an eagle   a mountain goat   an angel

1 to swim like _____

2 to sing like _____

3 to run up hills like _____

4 to eat like _____

5 to sleep like _____

4 Sentence correction ▶

Each of these sentences has a wrong verb form. Can you find it and correct it?

1 When the referee blew the whistle at the end of the game, neither team was scoring a single goal.

2 Did you ever won a big competition?

3 My bicycle had a puncture today although I was replacing the tyre last week.

4 Did Hala told you why she wasn't chosen for the team?

5 The child was in tears because he had fell off his bike.

6 Where have you bought your tennis racquet?

7 Dentists are taking care of people's teeth.

8 Last week I had twisted my ankle playing hockey.

5 Compound nouns ▶ SB p47

The following pairs of definitions contain one compound noun which is in common use, and one which is not normally used. Put a ✔ against the correct one, and a ✗ against the other. The first one has been done for you.

1 a man who delivers the post = a postman ✔
   a woman who cuts hair = a hairwoman   ✗

2 a diet to help you gain weight = a gaining diet
   a diet to help you slim = a slimming diet

3 a bag for carrying shopping home = a carrier bag
   a bag for taking papers to and from the office = a job bag

4 a cake made to celebrate winning a competition = a prize cake
   a cake made to celebrate a birthday = a birthday cake

5 a field for playing football on = a football pitch
   a field for camping on = a camping pitch

6 the place where people ice skate = an ice ring
   the area in which a boxing match takes place = a boxing ring

7 a young person who has just finished his/her schooling = a school leaver
   a young person who has recently left home to live independently = a home leaver

6 More compound nouns ▶   SB p47

Find a compound noun for each of these definitions. The first one has been done for you.

1 a court reserved specially for playing badminton
   a badminton court

2 a form you fill in when you apply for something
   _____

3 a shirt you wear to play football in
   _____

4 gloves boxers wear during a boxing match
   _____

5 special pads you wear over your shins to protect this part of your body during cricket
   _____

6 a stadium where spectators stand or sit to watch football matches
   _____

7 Newspaper headlines ▶   SB p49

Unjumble these headlines to make sense. Use a capital letter to begin the first word.

1 list novel tops romantic bestseller
2 weapon disease new against heart
3 of brink rare extinction whale species on
4 join glorious carnival fun in hundreds
5 in cancer mobile users scare phone
6 contract firm city wins jobs

8 Noun or verb? ▶   SB p49

Study each headline and decide whether the word in italics is being used as a noun or as a verb.

1 Company *markets* weight-loss product
2 City *markets* report trading loss
3 '*Profits* down again' says warehouse boss
4 'No-one will *profit* from Mick's death' declares dad
5 *Share* prices on the increase
6 Mum to *share* lottery win with kids
7 Minister *promises* tax benefits
8 'His *promises* meant nothing' heartbroken star reveals

9 Phrasal verbs in headlines ▶ SB p55

Newspaper headlines often contain phrasal verbs, or nouns formed from phrasal verbs.
Example: *Boxing shapes up for a comeback.*

Match each of these headlines with the correct short summary.

1 Shock as Freshfoods lays off 990

2 Shoplifter gets off without jail

3 'More cutbacks on way' warns Brown

4 Football star pulls out of deal

5 First lady stands by her man

6 Few take up job offer

7 School leavers miss out on training

8 Tennis queen heads for defeat

a The wife of the President of the United States is determined to stay loyal, despite recent rumours.

b A careers survey indicates that six out of seven employers fail to ensure that employees aged between 16 and 20 have the opportunity to pursue work-related qualifications.

c A man convicted of stealing £250 worth of goods from a sportswear shop has been given a suspended sentence.

d Jimmy Davis, who has been in the process of agreeing a contract with Stockport United for four million pounds, last night refused to continue with negotiations.

e The region's largest employer blames competition from a rival supermarket chain for the loss of almost a thousand jobs.

f The Minister of Education, speaking at a conference in Sutherland at the weekend, said that spending on schools and colleges is to be further reduced.

g Alice Foster, the current singles champion, has lost seven out of her eight matches in South Africa and is likely to lose her title.

h Only five employees, from a possible 32, have accepted new work contracts at the town's largest supermarket.

10 Vocabulary check ▶ SB pp52–53

Choose the correct word from each pair in italics.

1 Sasha wants to get fit and has booked a *consultation/confrontation* with a personal trainer.

2 Anna bought some long-sleeved *cloths/tops* to go with her new trousers.

3 The problems of *truancy/delinquency* at the school were resolved when careful checks on absence were introduced.

4 I got an eye injury when I was boxing and it is in *fear/danger* of becoming infected.

5 At 16, Harry enjoys similar music and activities to his *teenagers/peers*.

6 The sports club has put in a brand new tennis *ground/court*.

7 Do you think the new football captain has enough experience to *bring/take* command of the team?

8 The rules for taking part in the project were quite strict. Anyone breaking them could be *excluded/exported*.

9 I hope to *get/pass* a qualification in sports coaching.

11 Grammar and spelling ▶

The third person singular of a verb in the present simple ends in either *-s* or *-es*.
Examples: He *enjoys* cricket. He *tries* to improve his technique. Cricket *teaches* teamwork.

Put the verbs in these sentences into the present simple, using the correct spelling for each ending.

1 He (enjoy) playing musical instruments in his spare time and (approach) the playing of the violin like a professional.

2 The instructor always (stress) the importance of correct technique.

3 If that little boy (splash) or (punch) anyone again, he will have to get out of the water.

4 She (sing) at concerts and her husband (accompany) her on the guitar.

5 Is Mr Singh the man who (fix) car engines and (go) jogging in his spare time?

6 Nadia (try) hard and is sure to do well.

7 Why do you keep playing football with Dimitri if he never (pass) you the ball?

8 She usually (mash) food before giving it to her baby.

9 He (focus) on the game and never (worry) about losing.

10 If Lorenzo doesn't know the answer, he just (guess) and (hope) he's right.

12 Sentence correction ▶

Add the missing word in the right place in each of these sentences.

1 It isn't true that is always cold in Iceland.

2 The injured footballer taken to hospital by taxi.

3 If you're going shopping, I come too.

4 Plenty of good food and exercise is the key living a long and healthy life.

5 Learning squash was easier I expected.

6 If the racquet doesn't cost too much money, I buy it.

7 Aliki asked to borrow my swimming goggles, so I lent to her.

8 Are you concerned about the effects of pollution the environment?

13 Vocabulary check ▶   SB p55

Decide whether the following sentences make proper sense. Give each one a ✔ or a ✘.
Think carefully about the words in italics.

1 On holiday we stayed in a comfortable, *boarded-up* house.

2 You find a lot of rich people and expensive houses in *deprived areas* of town.

3 Someone is needed to *co-ordinate* all the sports matches we play with other schools.

4 Giving babies coffee instead of milk to drink is *beneficial* to them.

5 When Carmen arrived in Jordan she couldn't speak a word of Arabic and had to learn the language *from scratch*.

6 Cinema owners want to *reverse the decline* in cinema attendance.

7 Doctors are *sceptical* about the health benefits of good food and exercise.

14 Five-minute note-taking practice ▶ SB p56

Quickly read this article about a boxing club. Then complete the notes outlining the practical steps the owner has taken to ensure the club is a success. It is a good idea to underline the relevant points as you read.

Mike Foster is the owner of the successful Fairways Boxing Club, now in its second year. The early years were far from easy, though.

Mike admits he was worried at first about the lack of interest from the public. 'The main problem when we started the club,' he explained, 'was the perception of boxing as a dangerous sport which can result in head injuries.'

Parents in particular were worried, and the initial take-up of membership was very low. In order to change the poor image of boxing, Mike ran a radio campaign pointing out that anyone can take part in boxing, whatever their level of fitness or previous experience. Another marketing tool he has used is a video promoting non-contact boxing techniques, which he circulates to schools. These methods are paying off and the club is flourishing. Membership is up by 50% on last year, and girls as well as boys are becoming converts. Structured training courses have been specially devised for all levels of ability – from those starting from scratch to advanced level.

Although members of the medical profession remain sceptical about the safety of boxing, there is no doubt that the matches are carefully supervised. Furthermore, Mike insists that only friendly competition is allowed. Instructors have to be qualified before he employs them, and also trained in first aid.

Mike has gone to a lot of trouble to redecorate the club house. The attractive cream and blue painted changing rooms are fully equipped with hot showers, hairdryers, lockers and mirrors. 'I want members to feel proud of Fairways and to feel good about coming here,' Mike said.

1 _____

2 _____

3 _____

4 _____

5 _____

6 _____

7 _____

8 _____

9 _____

15 Five-minute summary writing ▶   SB p56

Working quickly, join your notes from exercise 14 into a paragraph. Try to use some of your own words where possible.

16 Using fewer words ▶   SB p56

Rewrite the sentences more concisely, using the words from the box. The first one has been done for you.

traumatic   nibbled   champion   chronic   co-educational
anxiety   painkiller   concentrate on

1 Please try to think about hitting the ball and not think about anything else at the same time.

   Please try to concentrate on hitting the ball.

2 Raul goes to a school where boys and girls are educated together.

3 He is a specialist in skin diseases which continue for a long time.

4 The car accident was a bad and frightening experience for my brother.

5 The person who won all the races was given a medal.

6 Marisa has a great deal of fear and uncertainty about the future.

7 The doctor gave the injured sportsman a type of medicine for relieving pain.

8 She took small bites from a chocolate biscuit while she drank her coffee.

17 Redundant words ▶   SB p56

Cross out the unnecessary words in these sentences. The first one has been done for you.

1 People say that participating ~~and taking part~~ in sport is more important than winning.

2 We cycled by bike to the lake of water.

3 Children sometimes hurt themselves falling over in the playground which is where they play their games during school breaks.

4 Our best football player is in hospital being treated for a sports injury that he got while playing sport.

5 After her operation, Emily had to keep to a fat-free diet and not eat any fat for three months.

6 I wore my new running shoes to run in when I took part in the competition.

7 Mr Scott believes in teamwork so he thinks everyone should work together as part of a team.

8 Are you looking for a swimming costume in a plain colour or a multi-coloured one in many different colours?

9 Lex Arnold, the famous boxer, has just written his own autobiography telling people his life story.

10 They want to promote the sport to schools throughout the country to enable it to be better recognised and known about.

18 Vocabulary check ▶   SB p59

Choose the correct word from each pair in italics.

1 Geraldine's *extended/extension* family all live in the same neighbourhood.

2 You don't have to *deprive/deny* yourself of good food in order to lose weight.

3 The idea of going on holiday and leaving their newborn baby with a nanny was *inconceivable/inconclusive*.

4 The taxi was delayed going to the airport and I was *distressing/panicking* because I thought we would miss the plane.

5 At the supermarket we got a *trolley/truck* for our shopping.

6 I look and feel better and have more *self-esteem/self-expression* since I lost weight.

7 Although she no longer goes to English classes, she is able to *maintain/prolong* her level of English by reading novels.

8 Alan was so tired after the day's work that he used to *slump/stumble* in front of the TV and do nothing all evening.

9 My friend Juan is so busy at school. He's taking lots of exams, is captain of the cricket team, and even *pushes/crams* in learning the violin at lunchtime.

19 Informal expressions ▶   SB p59

Choose the correct informal expression to complete each sentence.

| a new lease of life   got out of hand   keep clear of   hooked |
| got rid of   boost   snacked   nibbles |

1 Grandma used to be almost confined to the house but the new drugs to treat her arthritis have given her _____ .

2 The weeds in the garden _____ while we were away on holiday.

3 I loved learning jazz dance. After the first class, I was _____ .

4 I passed around the drinks and _____ when our party guests arrived.

5 Martin needs lots of reassurance and praise to _____ his morale.

6 We didn't have time for a proper meal so we _____ on cheese and biscuits.

7 She _____ all her old clothes and shoes by giving them to charity.

8 You need to _____ people who smoke if you are trying to give up smoking yourself.

20 Text completion ▶

Complete this text about a healthy diet by putting ONE word in each space.

These days, there is a great deal (1) _____ pressure to be slim and to reduce the amount of fat in our diet. Many slimming diets tell us to 'count calories', and fat certainly (2) _____ twice as many calories as protein. (3) _____ it is important to keep an eye on the amount of fat that we eat. A fast food meal of hamburger, fries and a milkshake typically contains 60 per cent fat, (4) _____ is excessive.

Unfortunately, however, many people now underestimate (5) _____ importance of eating some fat. A long-term fat-free diet (6) _____ have disastrous consequences for our levels of energy and our physical condition. In (7) _____ , a reasonable layer of fat is necessary to cover the body's skeleton. Cutting back (8) _____ calorie intake drastically and completely removing a wide range of foods (9) _____ the diet are dangerous. The long-term effects include bone thinning and muscle wastage.

Experts claim that the Mediterranean diet is (10) _____ of the healthiest in the world. It is rich (11) _____ olive oil and low in animal fats (butter, cheese, etc). Olive oil is thought to lower blood cholesterol levels (12) _____ absorbing fat in the bloodstream. The best advice is (13) _____ eat a varied diet from all the food groups daily, including protein, fats and carbohydrates. We should also remember that growing children need more calories in relation to their size (14) _____ adults.

21 Understanding pie charts ▶

Leyfield Leisure Centre analysed the popularity of the activities it offers to users. Study the pie chart, then complete the paragraph below.

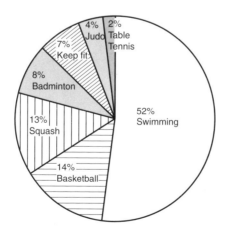

The most popular activity by far is (1) _____ and the least popular is (2) _____ . The second most popular activity is (3) _____ . Over a quarter of users of the Leisure Centre come to play (4) _____ and squash. Badminton is only a little ahead of (5) _____ in popularity, but it is twice as popular as (6) _____ .

UNIT 4 Transport Issues

1 Aeroplane vocabulary ▶ SB pp64–65

Add the missing letters to the incomplete words in these sentences.

1 The c_____ consisted of two pilots and eight flight attendants.

2 The pilot let us visit the c_____ and see all the plane's instruments.

3 In an emergency, the o_____ m_____ will help you breathe more easily.

4 The details of the plane's flight are recorded in the b_____ _____x.

5 Our tickets were checked and our b_____e was weighed when we checked in for our flight.

6 After the emergency landing, the passengers escaped from the plane by sliding down a c_____e.

7 The flight attendant demonstrated the use of the l_____ j_____s, which are to be used if the plane lands on water.

8 'What is that red cylinder for?' asked the little boy, pointing to the f_____ e_____r.

2 Choose the best word ▶ SB pp67–68

Choose the correct word to complete each sentence.

1 Experts say that the _____ of a serious air accident is one in two million.

 a opportunity   **b** certainty   **c** chance   **d** expectation

2 An aeroplane can also be called a plane or an _____ .

 a aircrew   **b** aircraft   **c** airmail   **d** airway

3 A plane's _____ depends, not on hours spent flying, but on the total number of journeys made.

 a lifeline   **b** lifestyle   **c** life history   **d** lifespan

4 The maintenance engineers inspected the crack and decided the plane was not _____ .

 a airless   **b** airworthy   **c** airborne   **d** airtight

5 Modern technology makes some aircraft _____ , and airlines usually replace these planes with more up-to-date models.

 a ageing   **b** useless   **c** obsolete   **d** obscure

6 In theory all countries which have signed the Chicago Convention operate to the same international safety standards, but in _____ this is not so.

 a really   **b** daily   **c** practice   **d** records

7 Because airlines operate _____ schedules, a delay on one flight often affects later flights.

 a tight   **b** small   **c** close   **d** narrow

8 Tiredness, boredom and long working hours put strain on pilots and can lead to pilot _____ .

 a accident   **b** crashes   **c** revolt   **d** error

3 Phrasal verbs with *take* ▶

Choose the correct ending from the box for each of these sentences. There is one more than you need.

> take them up   take away   took it off   taken out
> taken on   taken in   took off

1 After several delays the plane finally _____ .

2 The trousers were too big at the waist so I had them _____ .

3 Those curtains are too long for the windows. We need to _____ .

4 It was hot wearing a coat in the sunshine so she _____ .

5 As the level of production at the factory increased, more staff were

_____ .

6 Kevin's tooth was so painful that he went to the dentist and had it

_____ .

4 Logical reasoning ▶   SB p66

If ...(then) constructions are used to show how one thing depends on another.
Example: *If you're late for your flight, (then) the plane will leave without you.*
Notice the comma after the first clause.

Match the halves to make complete sentences.

1 If the weather is fine tomorrow,

2 If your aunt doesn't rest after her operation,

3 If pilots become overtired,

4 If you take this medicine for your cough,

5 If an airline attracts a lot of bad publicity,

6 If I go to bed late,

7 If the engineers can't repair the plane,

8 If scientific research into this rare virus is successful,

9 If Teresa earns some extra money,

10 If I fly with a charter airline,

a then deaths from the disease will be reduced.

b fewer passengers choose to fly with it.

c then I feel tired all the next day.

d she won't recover properly.

e then we'll go to the seaside.

f then she'll be able to buy some new clothes.

g you'll feel better in a few days.

h then air safety is put at risk.

i then it won't take off on time.

j then my ticket will be cheaper.

5 Sentence completion ▶   SB p66

Complete these sentences with a logical conclusion of your own.

1 If we finish our homework quickly, _____

2 If Omar doesn't take care of his teeth, _____

3 If you drink all the milk in the fridge tonight, _____

4 If global warming continues, _____

6 Linking words: Reason and consequence ▶   SB p66

Because and *as* are used to show reason. Example: *Charter flights are cheaper because the airlines sell their tickets wholesale to the tour operators.*

Use *because* or *as* to make complete sentences from these prompts.

1 skies getting more crowded/number flights made/increasing

2 parents not allow me/have motorcycle/too dangerous

3 swimming lessons cancelled/pool leaking

4 all planes/that type/grounded/engineers found severe fault/one model

As a result / Therefore / Consequently are all used to express logical consequence.
Example: *The charter airlines sell their tickets wholesale to the tour operators.*
As a result, their tickets are cheaper. (*So* means the same but is more informal.)

Write a logical consequence for each of these sentences. Use the prompts in brackets and one of the above expressions.

5 Engineers told the crew they did not want the plane to take off until it was passed as completely safe. (passengers/long delay)

6 There is a great deal of pressure to look good nowadays. (feel inadequate)

7 The pilot told passengers the fog was too thick to risk landing in London and … (land/Manchester)

8 Several new companies have opened up in our town. (house prices/rise)

7 Text correction ▶   SB p70

This leaflet was written by students for motorists and is aimed at making their town a better place to live. Read it carefully and correct the mistakes. There are a total of 14.

Speeding drivers

There are a lot dangerous drivers here and the culprit is you! You get up late on Monday, don't have time of breakfast and tear by the town breaking the speed limit. You could kill half a dozen students in their way to school! 33% of us now come to school by car. More on us would walk to school if the roads weren't so dangerous, so please slow down!

Car fumes

Are you driving a fuel-efficient model. When you need petrol, do you reach out the lead-free variety. It's not just school pupils who are suffering of asthma – so are adults. Cutting them down the car fumes will mean cleaner air for everyone.

Park and Ride

The new 'Park and Ride' system means you can now leave your car outside town and get to the centre quickly with bus. No-one likes sitting in traffic jams, so why aren't you using it.

Wildlife

Pollution contributes on acid rain which is harmful to wildlife. You can help protect our birds and wild creatures by not making unnecessary journeys in car.

8 Word formation ▶   SB pp71–73

Change each word in italics into its correct form.

1 Our cycle route took us through some *beauty* countryside.

2 Are the new roads really *necessity*?

3 Many people are happy to *donation* money to charity.

4 Jeremy had always wanted to *owner* a motorbike.

5 *Participate* in the teams will get free T-shirts.

6 You can *registration* for the ride on your own or with a group of friends.

7 Bicycles don't *pollution* the atmosphere.

8 Simple *refresh* such as soft drinks and biscuits are available during the breaks.

9 My father agreed to be a *sponsoring* when I took part in the cycle ride.

10 The trees, bushes and wild flowers are all part of the rich *diverse* of our countryside.

11 We used a map to *guidance* us through the centre of the city.

12 Environmental campaigns are very *popularity* with young people.

9 Grammar: Future simple in the passive voice ▶   SB p72

The form of the future simple in the passive voice is *will be* + past participle.
Example: *Sponsors will be entered in a prize draw.*

If it is important to know who/what the agent is, we use *by*.
Example: *The area will be split into two by the new motorway.*

The object of an active sentence becomes the subject of a passive sentence.
Example: *The development will increase pollution.* (active)
            Pollution will be increased by the development. (passive)

Try to change these active sentences into the passive form. Use *by* if necessary.

1 Someone will send participants an official sponsorship form.

    An official sponsorship form …

2 Experienced riders will guide you on the route.

    You …

3 Experts will plan the route of the cycle ride.

4 Increasing traffic fumes will damage children's health.

5 The campaign will highlight the threats to the surrounding area.

6 These funds will sustain the organisation's environmental campaign.

7 They will lay on extra trains.

8 A person will meet participants at the start of the route.

9 They will encourage people not to use cars.

10 Someone will give prizes to the teams.

10 'Walk to school' campaign ▶

Your school's environmental club has decided to start a campaign to encourage more students to walk to school rather than coming by car or bus. The notes below set out the arrangements for the campaign. Change each point into a sentence in the passive voice, using *will be* + past participle. The first one has been done for you.

1 Inform all students about campaign

All students will be informed about the campaign.

2 Publish article in school magazine

_____

3 Write letters to parents

_____

4 Tell students to walk in pairs or threes

_____

5 Ask senior students to look after junior pupils

_____

6 Use money saved on petrol and fares to improve school's cycle sheds

_____

11 Linking words: Addition and contrast ▶   SB p73

Moreover / Furthermore / In addition are used to add information to what has just been said. Example: *All aeroplanes are inspected before each flight. In addition, they have to undergo strict maintenance procedures.*

However and *Nevertheless* are used to introduce a contrasting idea. Example: *Cycling on busy roads can be dangerous. Nevertheless, it is an efficient and liberating way of travelling.*

Add a new sentence to each of the following, using the prompts in brackets. Begin your sentence with one of the above linking words and expressions. Think carefully about the meaning as you decide which type to use.

1 A large petrol company has decided not to open a petrol station in the village because the population is small and people's incomes are low. (most use bikes/get/work)

2 Riding a motorcycle is fast and exciting. (quite dangerous form/transport)

3 Surprisingly, air travel is the safest mode of transport. (many people say/scared/flying)

4 We were disappointed with our day out to the theme park. The tickets cost a lot of money and you had to pay extra for some of the attractions. (long queues/get on rides/ some rides not working)

5 If a factory were built in our village, young people would no longer have to leave the area to look for work. (factory/encourage more people/move into village/as a result/local shops/get more customers)

12 Presenting the pros and cons ▶   SB pp73–74

There is a proposal to build a factory in a beautiful area of countryside. A resident, Paula, has written to the local paper putting forward the pros and cons of the idea. Match the highlighted words and phrases in her letter with the following headings.

Listing *In the first place* _____

Contrast _____

Reasoning _____

Emphasis _____

Addition _____

Consequence _____

Opinion *I was delighted* _____

Summing up _____

Dear Editor,

I was delighted when I heard of the proposal to build a new furniture factory *because* we really need more jobs in this area. If a factory were built in Kemble, our economic future would be secure and young people *in particular* would no longer have to leave the area to look for work. I realise there are a number of problems concerned with the proposal *but* these could be overcome.

In the first place, it has been pointed out that there is no access road to the site where the proposed factory would be built. *In my view, however,* a new road to the factory could be constructed by cutting through the wood that surrounds the village.

Secondly, the factory would encourage more people to move into Kemble, resulting in increased pressure on housing. *However*, a block of flats could be built on the edge of the village, where the recreation ground is now. *Therefore* I think the overcrowding objection can be answered.

Another point to consider is that a bigger population has many advantages. The village shop would have more customers, for example. *As a result*, it could expand and offer a better range of goods. *Moreover*, the local school would get more pupils. *Consequently* more teachers and better resources would probably be made available.

On balance I think we should definitely go ahead with the new factory *as surely* all these advantages outweigh any disadvantages that people might be concerned about.

Yours faithfully,

Paula Marconi

13 Word game ▶

Add one extra letter to each of these words to make a new word connected with transport or travel.

1 plot   an exciting job for someone   *pilot*

2 rod   you travel along this   _____

3 hat   another word for stop   _____

4 lane   a good way to travel   _____

5 tip   a kind of journey   _____

6 ton   smaller than a city   _____

7 are   region   _____

8 crow   large group   _____

9 rain   faster than a car   _____

10 sin   this one showed us where the toilets were   _____

14 Understanding graphs ▶

Study the graph showing ticket sales of two low-cost airlines, Quickjet and Fly Now. Then answer the questions below.

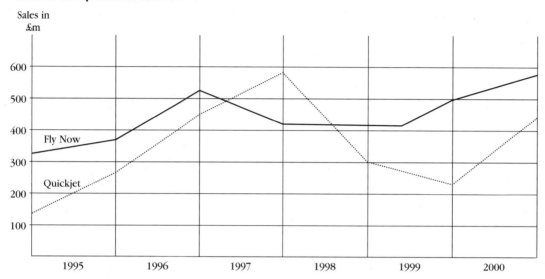

1   What was the value of Quickjet sales for the year 1996?

2   In which year did Quickjet sales drop sharply?

3   Which was the best year for Fly Now sales?

4   How much was earned from Fly Now sales in 1999?

5   In which year did Quickjet sales exceed those of Fly Now?

15 Choose the best word ▶   SB pp76–77

Choose the correct word to complete each sentence.

1   The new shopping centre will bring many _____ to the town.

   a benefits   **b** boosts   **c** assistance   **d** pleasure

2   We went by boat and train on our _____ to Spain.

   a travel   **b** transport   **c** journey   **d** voyage

3   Since the _____ was built, we no longer have heavy traffic thundering through the town centre.

   a byway   **b** by-election   **c** bypass   **d** by-law

4   The idea that a new swimming pool will not cost much to build is _____ .

   a debating   **b** insensible   **c** ludicrous   **d** pernicious

5   The storm brought trees down, ripped roofs off houses and did all kinds of _____ to the town.

   a damage   **b** deterioration   **c** decay   **d** despair

6   After losing several matches, our team was _____ from the competition.

   a missed   **b** lost   **c** eliminated   **d** elapsed

7   Eleni bought a bicycle to try to _____ the amount of money she was spending on transport to college.

   a save   **b** reduce   **c** less   **d** lower

8 It's best to avoid travelling during busy periods as the roads are so _____ .

    a congealed   **b** overfilled   **c** congested   **d** occupied

9 Layla was worried that the pain in her arm might be serious, but tests showed that her fears were _____ .

    a undone   **b** unthinkable   **c** unobtainable   **d** unfounded

10 My father works in an office a long way from home and so he spends a lot of time _____ to work.

    a time-wasting   **b** commuting   **c** transporting   **d** waiting

16 Relating to your target audience ▶   SB p78

Match the extracts below with the following target audiences.

Internet users _____   Teenage magazine readers _____   Parents _____

Residents _____   People looking for a job _____   A penfriend _____

A In our business, we always put our customers first. If you share this approach, please get in touch as we have a number of exciting career openings now available.

D We have noticed that a number of people, when dropping their children off at school or collecting them, are driving out along the 'in' road for a quick getaway. This is dangerous, so please keep to the one-way system.

B It was wonderful hearing about life on your farm. You may think looking after the animals is a bit dull, but I'd love to change places with you.

E I adore fashion but I think there's too much pressure on young people to buy the latest styles. Every month, we read articles like yours which insist that a new style is in and the outfit we bought last season is out.

C Cinemas, sports events, concerts … this database is a treasure trove of invaluable information. Once registered with the site, you'll receive regular e-news, bringing you up to date with the latest special offers.

F A number of rumours have been circulating about the proposed developments in the locality. I hope that the meeting will allow each homeowner to be better informed about the situation.

17 Paragraphing and punctuation ▶

Add the punctuation and paragraphing to this article for a school newsletter. Don't forget to read it through first to get the sense.

recently our class held a fund-raising disco barbecue and we decided after some disagreement to donate the funds to the local hospital some students argued that the school needed the money to replace our ageing computers however in my opinion we made the right decision to donate the money to a good cause although the organising the event was hard work and time consuming I think most of us enjoyed selling the tickets and cooking the food in addition the nurses told us our donation helped buy oxygen cylinders for emergency use which made us feel very proud whats more important anyway a state-of-the-art computer or saving lives nevertheless some students still disagree and I understand their point of view on balance I think that although most of our fund-raising efforts should continue to benefit local charities we should have one event each year just for our school then we could get rid of obsolete stuff like the old typewriters and buy up-to-date equipment what do the rest of you think Id love to know your views

18 Linking words round-up ▶

The following text is part of a school newsletter article. Complete each section in the most appropriate way.

Do you ever get fed up with tripping over bits of wire and old drink cans, and bumping into dog walkers, while you are trying to enjoy a game of basketball? Well I've got good news for you! The council has offered us some money for a new recreation area instead of the waste ground where we play now. It's going to be properly surfaced and provided with benches and a shelter.

a   Nevertheless, dog walkers will probably object to the idea.

b   In addition, a high fence will be built around it to keep stray dogs out.

c   Moreover, we will have to raise some of the funds ourselves.

d   So no-one will drop litter there again.

The new area will be open to anyone who wants to use it.

e   As a result the gates will be locked after dark.

f   Consequently we can play safely without scrambling over weeds or broken glass.

g   On the other hand, crying babies in their pushchairs will no longer be in the way.

h   It will be unsupervised, however, so it will be unsuitable for young children.

I think some local people feel that improving the Old People's Centre is a more important priority than having a better recreation area.

i   Therefore the Old People's Centre would cost much more to improve.

j   However, I for one am delighted that for once young people have been the first consideration.

k   So unfortunately the old people will have to wait quite a long time for better facilities.

l   Moreover, teenagers will take good care of their new facility.

The bad news is that we are going to have to raise some of the money for the project ourselves and the council will provide the rest. We're already buzzing with loads of exciting ideas for fund-raising, including a grand summer dance. There'll be a meeting next Tuesday to discuss all the issues.

m   To sum up, I hope I have a chance to talk to everyone about these ideas.

n   On balance, the fund raising effort is going to be worth it.

o   So come along and add some ideas of your own. We can't wait to hear from you.

That's Entertainment!

1 Film vocabulary ▶ SB p84

Choose the correct word from each pair in italics.

1 With her beautiful looks and charming manner, Despina made a perfect romantic *heroine/hero*.

2 Who designed the *dresses/costumes* for the screen adaptation of 'Macbeth'?

3 I prefer to check the *reviews/text* of a film before deciding whether to see it.

4 A famous Hollywood actress has the starring role, while less well-known actors and actresses make up the rest of the *cast/group*.

5 There were so many different *figures/characters* in the film, I found it very confusing.

6 If the first *scene/section* in a film doesn't grab his attention, he quickly loses interest.

7 Comedy, tragedy and romance are examples of different *styles/genres*.

8 The film was so popular, there was a long queue for tickets outside the *box office/auditorium*.

2 More film vocabulary ▶ SB pp84–85

Add the missing letters to the incomplete words in these sentences.

1 The thriller we went to see had many sp_____ e_____s, including a very realistic earthquake.

2 The best actors and actresses of the year receive O_____s in a prize-giving ceremony in Hollywood.

3 The film had many exotic s_____ngs, including a luxury ship, a desert island and an Arabian palace.

4 In the school play, all the children, even the youngest, were given a r_____e to play.

5 I was in terrible s_____nse because I wasn't sure if the heroine would be rescued before the ship sank.

6 The cartoon did not have an important m_____ge about the meaning of life, but it made the children laugh a lot.

7 I think Tom Cruise is a powerful actor but I found his p_____nce in his latest film rather disappointing.

8 I wouldn't re_____d this horror film for young children. It's too frightening.

9 . She is quite a good actress but I don't think she will ever be a real s_____r.

3 *So ... that* and *such ... that* ▶ SB p85

Add an adjective or an adjective + noun to complete these sentences. Don't use *nice* or *good*!

1 It was such a(n) _____ _____ that she won the Oscar for 'best actress'.

2 It was such a(n) _____ _____ that I had to read on to the end.

3 I thought he was such a(n) _____ _____, I can't wait to see his next film.

4 Jack is so _____ in the role of romantic hero that I almost fell in love with him.

5 The battle scene was so _____, I was glad I was with my best friends.

6 The tragic ending was so _____, I felt exhausted by the end.

7 There was such a _____ queue for tickets that I gave up and went home.

8 The soundtrack was so _____ that Demis went out the next day and bought the CD.

9 Watching the goodbye scene is so _____, you should prepare for tears.

4 Word formation ▶   SB pp86–87

Use the words in the box to form new words to complete the passage. The first one has been done for you. Use each word once only.

atmospheric entertaining emotion alive response substitution loneliness exciting perform

Is cinema better than theatre?

No!

Theatre is much better than cinema, or films on video or DVD, because it's (1) __*live*__ . From the minute you get inside the theatre, you can feel the (2) _____ and anticipation of the audience. The actors are there in front of you - living, breathing people speaking out the words and (3) _____ to laughter and clapping from the audience. Each theatrical (4) _____ is unique and special. This makes the (5) _____ very intense. When an actor cries on stage you see real tears, which makes the effect extremely (6) _____ . In my view, watching a film is a poor (7) _____ for a live performance and videos, in particular, are making society (8) _____ and passive. Next time you want some (9) _____ , give the theatre a go. You'll have a great night out!

Now do the same with the following passage.

imagine power isolate express convenience direct

Is cinema better than theatre?

Yes!

Cinema is much more (10) _____ than theatre, in my opinion. For one thing, films can use special effects, camera tricks, and sound, and can zoom in on the actors' (11) _____ , so you know exactly how they are feeling. In the theatre, you need to rely on the dialogue and your own (12) _____ . In films, the (13) _____ can ask for as many takes as necessary to get a polished performance. As an alternative to going to the cinema, renting a video can be good value. And it's certainly not making us more (14) _____ in our own homes. You can watch a video with friends, see it several times and pause it where you want, which means it's also very (15) _____ .

5 Collocations ▶   SB p87

Decide which of the nouns in the box can follow the adjectives below. Sometimes more than one noun is possible.

| furnishings   animation   ghost movie   documentary   shoes   murder |

stylish _____

atmospheric _____

witty _____

violent _____

thought-provoking _____

sumptuous _____

skilful _____

6 Odd word out ▶   SB p87

Cross out the adjective which doesn't sound right at the end of this sentence.

'In my opinion, this film shouldn't be missed – it's really impressive / magnificent / superb / memorable / enjoyable / sumptuous / absorbing.'

7 Describing films ▶   SB p87

Match the halves to make complete sentences.

1 Mesmerising special effects and a gripping plot make this latest Star Wars movie …

2 The spine-chilling opening scene had us all …

3 If you like witty dialogue and hilarious situations, …

4 We thought the quirky cartoon characters …

5 During the heart-rending and poignant final scene, …

6 When the ruthless and bloodthirsty gangsters are finally captured by the police, …

7 Although the plot was rather slow-moving and predictable, …

8 The sumptuous costumes and dazzling settings of this historical royal romance …

9 This thought-provoking and well-made drama tells the troubling tale …

a this enjoyable comedy will be just right for you.

b were both original and engaging.

c will transport you back to the beauty and grace of an earlier age.

d you won't be able to hold back the tears.

e a must for science fiction fans everywhere.

f of a boy forced into a life of poverty and deceit.

g the skilful performances more than compensated for it.

h sitting on the edge of our seats with suspense.

i we all breathed a deep sigh of relief.

8 Describing plots ▶   SB p88

The action of a film is told mainly in the present tense. Read these plot descriptions and correct any mistakes in the verb tenses. Some of the texts have one mistake, and some have two.

1 After her mother dies in a tragic accident, Annie decides to go her own way in search of romance and fulfilment. She starts a job in a new city and meets Max, a taxi driver with a difference. Max introduced Annie to his world and friendship blossoms.

2 An earthquake, a mud slide and an aeroplane crash… this latest James Bond movie has the most mesmerising special effects yet. Bond (Pierce Brosnan) investigates a rogue CIA agent and a fantastic speedboat chase follows. The agent wants to exact revenge and Bond is forced to defend himself anyway he can. Everything within arm's reach has become a weapon – even sharks!

3 Long-suffering dad Harold leaves his dull job in Texas to begun a new career in Manhattan with his son, Danny, an aggressive and ill-mannered teenager. Relations between father and son deteriorate until dad needs the money for a life-saving heart operation. It's up to Danny to save his life – but can he done it?

4 Julia Roberts portrays Susie, a chef with no common sense. Susie inherits her aunt's restaurant, then nearly ruined it. Enter meek bank clerk Tony, who is detecting the real problems behind the business and takes Susie under his wing.

5 Vicente is a rich city playboy intent on fulfilling his innermost wishes and desires. Life changes when he travels to the country to take over his grandfather's farm. Vicente hates rural life, so when farmgirl Zoe has fallen in love with him, rejection and tragedy result.

6 Tom loses his four-year-old daughter Kerry in a crowded supermarket. Despite desperate police searches, Kerry is never found. Then one day, ten years later, a girl knocked on the door. Could this be Kerry? And if so, why did she have no memory of her family?

7 The crew of a submarine are almost at the bottom of the ocean when the engine room caught fire. Can superhero Bruce reach them in time? There is no margin for error in this tense rescue mission that will defy all the odds.

9 Choose the best word ▶   SB pp91–92

Choose the correct word or phrase to complete each sentence.

1 I was surprised at how well the children could _____ modelling clay when they made the puppets for their theatre performance.

   a touch **b** handle **c** hold **d** move

2 The teacher told Lili that, although her ideas were good, the spelling errors in her work showed a real lack of _____ .

   a good grades **b** attention to detail **c** careless mistakes **d** poor progress

3 Osman turned down party invitations, theatre tickets and other distractions, and devoted himself _____ to passing his exams.

   a single-mindedly **b** desperately **c** skilfully **d** ruthlessly

4 An animator has to build up his or her work frame by frame. Each film takes a very long time to make, and so _____ are essential to see the project through to the end.

   a research and development **b** continuity and relaxation
   c diversions and rewards **d** dedication and commitment

5 The artist said that she spent a lot of time watching people, and that her
_____ were the main reason she was able to paint
people in such a lifelike way.

a interpersonal skills   **b** artistic gifts   **c** natural talents
d powers of observation

6 The set designer was very annoyed that his name was not on the _____
which appeared at the end of the film.

a list of credits   **b** scriptwriting   **c** director's fee   **d** full-length feature

7 The famous photographer's long beard, unusual clothes and strange lifestyle led many
people to describe him as a(n) _____ character.

a embittered   **b** eccentric   **c** revengeful   **d** likeable

8 When I first began writing poetry, I think the poets that I had studied at school
_____ my approach and the things I wrote about.

a communicated   **b** impressed   **c** influenced   **d** discussed

10 Prepositions ▶

Complete each sentence with the correct preposition.

1 The film-maker talked to us _____ his early career.

2 When I was younger, I had no interest _____ reading historical novels.

3 Have you ever seen her perform _____ public?

4 The film was based _____ a true story.

5 The part of the villain was played _____ an unknown actor.

6 I don't agree that too many films come out _____ Hollywood.

7 The autobiography provided a rewarding insight _____ the singer's family
background.

8 The film is set _____ a remote island in the Pacific.

9 Not all jobs _____ the film industry are as glamorous as people think.

11 Choose the best word ▶   SB p95

Complete each sentence by choosing the correct word or phrase.

1 Small children need to learn to _____ between reality and fantasy.

a discriminate   **b** discern   **c** determine   **d** detect

2 She was disappointed by the novel as the main characters seemed very _____.

a thin   **b** slight   **c** shallow   **d** small

3 I prefer an intriguing plot, rather than a _____ one where I can guess the
ending.

a predictable   **b** dramatic   **c** secure   **d** gripping

4 Apparently the thieves knew that the family had expensive jewellery in the house.
The police think this was the main _____ behind the burglary.

a excuse   **b** motive   **c** need   **d** intent

5 The anti-smoking campaign on TV used _____, such as showing terrible deaths from smoking-related diseases.

   a painful illness   **b** shock tactics   **c** medical care   **d** expert information

6 Many parents read to young children in order to _____ them mentally.

   a arouse   **b** grow   **c** enlarge   **d** stimulate

7 Marianne enjoys _____ pursuits like writing poetry, making clothes and playing the guitar.

   a creative   **b** imaginary   **c** intellectual   **d** physical

12 Text completion ▶

Complete this text about the future of reading for pleasure by putting ONE word in each space.

Many people claim that the twenty-first century will see the end of buying novels and reading (1) _____ pleasure. They say that reading (2)_____ dull and old-fashioned compared (3) _____ other kinds (4) _____ more sophisticated entertainment. Modern technology, as we know, is constantly making amusements such (5) _____ computer games and videos more and more compelling. (6) _____ , the development of the Internet also means that even (7) _____ you do want to read novels, you can do so electronically (8) _____ e-books. Consequently, there will be no need to have even (9) _____ single book in your house. It's hard (10) _____ believe, however, that everyone will want to give (11) _____ the pleasure of browsing through a cosy bookshop on a rainy afternoon. It's easier to (12) _____ a paperback to the beach than it is to take a computer (13) _____ you want some pleasant holiday reading. Books make ideal presents, too, and are much more exciting to unwrap (14) _____ an 'Internet token' or whatever the equivalent will be.

13 Sentence correction ▶

Add the missing word in the right place in each of these sentences.

1 Our visit to town to buy the latest 'Harry Potter' novel was a waste time as all the shops had sold out.

2 My cousin's school marks are always better mine.

3 Research shown that even babies enjoy being read to.

4 The novel is about a young boy growing in a poor family in New York.

5 Do TV programmes really make children think violence fun?

6 Some people say children have no right privacy, but I don't agree.

7 Our class is going to have discussion about the right age to get married.

8 His broken leg meant that he was able to walk a long way.

9 Chen's parents died when he was young and his aunt brought him.

10 Children who good at maths usually enjoy their maths lessons.

11 My house is not as big yours.

12 Is reading story really just as much fun as watching a video?

14 Understanding pie charts ▶

Study the pie chart, produced by a public library, which shows the kinds of books borrowed over a twelve-month period. Decide if the six statements are true or false. Then write two more sentences of your own.

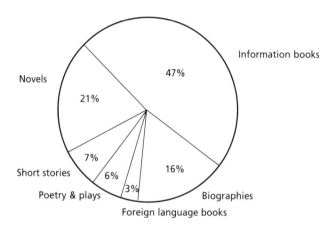

1 Novels were the most popular kind of book borrowed from the library.

2 More collections of short stories were borrowed than books of poetry and plays.

3 Fewer biographies were borrowed than information books.

4 Three times as many novels were borrowed as books of short stories.

5 Books in foreign languages were the least popular.

6 Over half of all books borrowed were information books.

15 Vocabulary check ▶   SB p97

Choose the correct word from each pair in italics.

1 Rania's gentle and *compassionate/passionate* nature was a wonderful asset in her job as a children's nurse.

2 He is well-known for his *integrity/dignity* and will always do what he believes is right, even if others don't agree.

3 'Tell me about your hopes and *inspirations/aspirations* for the future,' said the careers advisor.

4 I asked Hayley if she would *borrow/lend* me her copy of 'Great Expectations' when she had finished with it.

5 I found I could easily *associate/identify* with the heroine of the novel.

6 The joke was so funny that I *broke/burst* out laughing.

7 There were so many *ups and downs/twists and turns* in the plot that I lost the thread halfway through.

8 Joseph's parents didn't want him to leave the simple life on the farm and be exposed to the *corrosive/corrupting* influences of a big city.

9 Mr Badawi is quick to criticise his secretary. However, he does nothing to correct his own *shortcomings/short-changing*.

16 Writing in a more mature style ▶

1-10 below are extracts from students' film and book reviews. Match them with comments a-j, written in a more mature style.

1   I think this story that I got from the library is the one that I like the most because it is a good story and better than other stories that I have read all the time from the library.

2   I liked the things about life years and years ago in history times because it is not how life is now in modern days, but the people in this book are not like real people.

3   When you finally get to the end of this very long and very difficult book, you will feel sad about the people in it.

4   I think this film made me laugh a lot at the funny things the people in it do and I definitely think there are some things you will laugh a lot at when you see it too.

5   The acting is good but all of the people are dying and being killed all the time in this film by bad people who carry guns in their coats and pockets.

6   You go to a lot of nice places in the world in this film like a beach. But in my own real opinion, the film's story is not one that you can believe is true like other films.

7   I really think the lady who wrote this book whose name I forget, really did her best at writing it.

8   The only person you will like in this book is a young guy who has a new job which he gets because he wants to be a policeman as a career. He is a nice person and you will like him very much but he always believes things that even those bad guys in the book are telling him.

9   You want to read on more and more with this book because you want to know what is going to happen to the people in it because you cannot guess what is going to happen to them even when you are reading it.

10   When I read the book the main gentleman in the book is 18 at the beginning of the book and he is 19 at the end of the book. And when I went to see the film about the book the gentleman in it looked about 30 or 31 years of age. That was much too old than he should have been to be really like he was in the book.

a   It's the most gripping and moving story I have ever read.

b   In the screen adaptation of the novel, the hero looks too old for the part.

c   Although the locations are exotic, the plot is too far-fetched.

d   The author's technical skill is superb.

e   The suspense is great.

f   The most hard-hearted reader will be moved to tears in the final scenes of this 600-page classic.

g   The hero is a likeable but naive trainee police cop.

h   The performances were skilful but the violence was too bloodthirsty for my taste.

i   The comic scenes are so hilarious you'll have trouble holding on to your popcorn.

j   Although I enjoyed the nineteenth-century setting, the characters were not really convincing.

17 Language round-up ▶

Decide whether the following sentences make proper sense and give them either a ✓ or a ✗.

1   The writer was most disappointed to stay at the top of the bestseller list.

2   You'll be riveted by the slow and predictable plot.

3   A heart surgeon has no margin for error when performing an operation.

4   Jason decided to make his own way in life by following in his father's footsteps.

5   The most memorable cartoon characters often have a quirky appearance.

6   The extremely large and spacious dining room had everything within arm's reach.

7   We have very witty new furniture at home.

8   We were thrilled by the bland special effects in the adventure movie we went to see.

9   Vicki enjoyed being the target of constant harassment from the other pupils.

10   The wildlife series was made on location at the local film studio.

11   We easily found our way through the underground labyrinth.

12   The injured mountaineer, who had fallen down the cliff, defied the odds by surviving for ten days before he was rescued.

13   Mentally unstable people may need the care of a psychiatrist.

14   Her rebellious attitude made her very unpopular with the teachers at school.

15   His overconfident and brash image made him the perfect choice to portray the compassionate doctor in this Second World War film.

1 Vocabulary check ▶ SB p105

Complete each gap with a suitable word or phrase from the box. Be careful – there are two more than you need!

| culture and customs | nightlife | holiday resort | tourism |
| fully-equipped campsite | scenery | brochures | activities |

1   It can be hard staying in a tent if it rains, so we felt lucky to be staying on a(n) _____ which had hot showers, washing machines and a shop.

2   We looked at the holidays in lots of glossy _____ before choosing to go to Cyprus last summer.

3   The country we visited was so different from our own that at first we couldn't understand the way of life. Gradually, however, we got to know the people and came to appreciate their _____ .

4   The town we live in is also a popular _____ with a lovely beach and many places of entertainment for tourists.

5   Amalia's village is quiet and peaceful, with no clubs, discos or any other kind of _____ .

6   Our area is rather flat and uninteresting so we usually want to see mountains, lakes and other kinds of interesting _____ on holiday.

2 Paragraphing and punctuation ▶ SB pp106–107

Add the punctuation and paragraphing to this article about the ways holiday brochures achieve their persuasive effects. Don't forget to read it through first to get the sense.

recently our class looked at a brochure advertising an activity holiday we identified the persuasive techniques advertisers use to convince potential customers to choose this kind of holiday firstly we looked at the glossy photographs showing young people doing interesting activities the activities looked very appealing and succeeded in the advertisers aim of making us want to find out more about the holidays the target group for this kind of holiday is teenagers and we noticed how in order to increase a sense of identification young people of similar ages and backgrounds to ourselves were chosen for the pictures we also studied the information given in the brochure this was also persuasive as comments such as every minute of the day is filled with fun were cleverly smuggled in to look like real facts rather than just the advertisers opinions i think by choosing scenic locations happy-looking people and exciting activities the holiday company achieved their aim of making the holiday seem attractive in addition they cleverly disguised any negative aspects of the holiday if you are thinking of using holiday brochures remember the advertiser wants you to buy the holiday and will only show its good points so think of its potential drawbacks for yourself before making your mind up

3 Text completion ▶   SB pp109–110

This report, about the advantages and disadvantages of two different physical activities, appeared in a teenage magazine. Complete the gaps by reading for meaning and choosing from the vocabulary below. There is one extra word in each box.

lifesaving	sensitive	risky	supervised	shallow	warnings	sea
emergency	costume	suppleness	trunks	exercise	strain	

Next to football and cycling, swimming is one of the most popular activities. It develops stamina, (1) _____ and strength. It's good for people at all levels of fitness, as it doesn't place any (2) _____ on the joints. It's simple to arrange, it's not expensive and the only equipment you need is a(n) (3) _____ or a pair of (4) _____ .

The best places for swimming are (5) _____ public pools, although the high levels of chlorine used can be unpleasant. If your eyes are (6) _____ to chlorine, wearing goggles is recommended. Swimming in lakes, rivers or the sea can be exhilarating but is also (7) _____ . You should always obey red flag (8) _____ and be aware of tides and currents that can drag you out to (9) _____ . Never dive in (10) _____ water, as this can lead to serious injury.

As your swimming skills increase, you can think about taking (11) _____ certificates which will prepare you for any (12) _____ in water.

cracked	map reading	escape	balance	skid	flexible
invest	gates	erosion	compass	distances	

Mountain biking is an extremely exciting and fast-growing leisure activity. It's (13) _____ as you can do it in groups, in pairs or alone. It's not cheap, however, as you'll need to (14) _____ in a mountain bike and a suitable safety helmet before your first trip.

Mountain biking helps you develop skills, such as (15) _____ and using a (16) _____ . In fact, navigation skills are essential if you're thinking of biking over longer (17) _____ , as it's quite easy to become hopelessly lost. Mountain biking can also be dangerous, as you can (18) _____ on wet ground or lose your (19) _____ on a fast, rocky descent. So remember to wear that safety helmet at all times. It's better to have a (20) _____ helmet than a serious head injury!

Don't forget to look out for the environment, too. Never bike over crops, and always make sure you close (21) _____ behind you so that animals can't (22) _____ .

4 Position of adverbs ▶

Put the adverbs in brackets into the correct position in this paragraph. It was written by a student who has been working at a summer camp for children.

I've finished a hectic summer working as a camp helper at a summer camp near Seattle (just). No-one goes straight home when the camp closes and I'm no exception (ever, certainly). I've got plans to travel right across America, staying for a few days in any place that takes my fancy (sometimes). I'll feel exhausted by the time I get back to college but it's going to be worth it (probably, definitely). Although our wages were low, I saved a little every week for the trip and I did odd jobs for extra pay (occasionally).

5 Sentence correction ▶

In each of these sentences there is one extra word which shouldn't be there. Find it and cross it out.

1   The holiday was like nothing I had experienced before and I get a great delight every time I look through my photograph album.

2   I want to visit the Netherlands, the Balearic Islands, the France and the Czech Republic when I travel to Europe this summer.

3   Although they were exhausted when they reached at the top of the mountain, they had a marvellous sense of achievement and a wonderfully panoramic view.

4   Medical experts all over the world now agree that smoking it causes diseases of the lungs and heart.

5   The campsites are usually situated there in areas of outstanding natural beauty many miles from the nearest town.

6   I am going to go on an adventure holiday next summer because I will want more from a holiday than just a suntan.

7   Kurt had never done winter sports before and the skiing instructor explained him the differences between cross-country and downhill skiing.

6 Grammar revision ▶

Read this student's description of hiking and choose the correct word or phrase from each pair in italics.

I adore *being/to be* in the fresh air and I have belonged to a hiking club *from/since* I was fourteen. I particularly enjoy *exploring/to explore* little-known areas of countryside *where/which* nature still seems wild and untouched. I've learned a lot about wildlife and have succeeded in *identifying/to identify* many rare birds and delicate wild flowers. I usually take a camera or sketch book so that I can *capture/to capture* these moments, and I get great pleasure *from looking/to look* at the pictures afterwards. Sights such as spotting a wily fox emerging from his lair give me *a/one* particular thrill. Walking home in the evenings when the stars look *like/as though* jewels in the night sky is wonderful too. Hiking is a great pastime for people *they/who* need a relaxing outdoor activity *it/which* provides companionship and pleasant exercise without pressure or competition.

7 Expanding notes into sentences ▶   SB pp110–111

Turn these notes about a camping holiday into complete sentences by adding any necessary words, e.g. verbs, linking words, articles. The first one has been done for you.

1   arrived campsite – plan to stay few days
   We arrived at the campsite where we plan to stay for a few days.

2   fishing in nearby lake – didn't catch anything

3   caught in thunderstorm – no coats – soaked to skin

4   to country market – bought brand new CD dirt cheap

5   terrific walk through pine-scented forest – picnic near waterfall

6   met man in forest – lent us binoculars to look at wild boar

7   whole hour watching stupendous sunset – sky completely dark

8 'Body' idioms ▶

Complete each sentence with an idiomatic expression from the box. There is one more than you need.

> behind his back   tight-fisted   bite his tongue   keep a straight face
> off my chest   butterflies in my stomach   long in the tooth   itchy feet

1   The sales assistant got annoyed when the customer kept changing her mind about buying the shoes, but he had to _____ and say nothing.

2   Mr Chavez told his secretary she couldn't work on the project, but she went _____ and started work on it anyway.

3   Although he has plenty of money, my brother Oscar is very _____ and never buys anyone a present.

4   I hate speaking in front of a large group. In fact I get _____ just thinking about it.

5   I write down all my worries in a diary. I find it is a good way to get problems _____ .

6   Although the children wanted to be taken seriously when they talked about their pets, they made such funny mistakes that their teacher found it hard to _____ .

7   As soon as she has returned from one holiday, Maureen wants to abroad again. She must have been born with _____ .

9 Adjective suffixes ▶   SB p112

Fill the gaps with adjectives formed from the nouns in brackets. Add either *–able*, *–ic*, *–ous* or *–worthy*. Remember that adding a suffix can mean spelling changes too.

1   The most _____ part of our trip was the visit to the Roman ruins. (memory)

2   Not all snakes are _____ , you know. Some are completely harmless. (poison)

3   The island's _____ scenery and _____ weather made up for the rather _____ accommodation. (drama, glory, base)

4 Make sure your bicycle is _____ before starting a long journey. (road)

5 The weather on Cephalonia can be _____ in the autumn. (change)

6 The boat sank because it wasn't _____ . (sea)

7 The rescuers were awarded medals for their _____ act. (courage)

8 We rented a wonderfully _____ apartment with a _____ view of the bay. (space, panorama)

---

10 Text completion ▶   SB p113

Read this article about eco-tourism and choose the correct word or phrase from each pair in italics.

Eco-tourism is a fast-growing form of tourism which *arranges/gives* trips to little-known regions of the world such as the Namibian desert or the Malaysian rainforest.

According to/Regarding eco-tourist organisations, their approach avoids many of the drawbacks associated *to/with* ordinary tourism. Eco-tourists *observe/recognise* birds and animal behaviour, *study/learn* plant life, use canoes in preference *of/to* motorboats, live with local inhabitants rather than in hotels and *do/make* everything possible not to *interfere/disturb* the natural environment.

However, the opponents of eco-tourism *disagree/argue* that it is no better than conventional tourism. They say that it is introducing tourism into areas *when/where* there is a *fragile/fragmented* eco-system, and that the effect of large numbers of tourists *to/on* these environments is *even/further* more devastating. Eco-tourism companies are criticised *for/of* exploiting nature *in order/so* to provide tourists with cheap and easy thrills.

---

11 Building a letter from prompts ▶   SB pp114–115

Esther recently visited the Italian islands of Sicily and Sardinia. Build up a complete letter about her trip from these prompts.

Dear Nancy,

Just quick line/tell you about/our wonderful holiday/touring/beautiful islands/Sicily and Sardinia. They be places/I never go to/but always want/visit. Sicily be/astonishingly unspoiled. It have/grand but turbulent past. We see/traces Arabic and Greek influences/in dramatically-decorated buildings/ruined temples/we visit. We spend two nights/capital Palermo/which be throbbing/life. We also hire bicycles/and cycle/sleepy villages. We be/impressed/gentle pace/life/warmth/country people.

Sardinia be wild/untamed. Highlight/trip/be picnic/magical mountain setting. We sit/flower-studded meadow/near sparkling stream. Far below/we glimpse/Mediterranean/gleam/like blue jewel/in sunshine. In sky above/hawks circle/and only sound/be rustling/wind/trees.

It be/holiday/I never forget.

Write soon/tell me/news.

Love,

Esther

12 Understanding maps ▶   SB pp114–115

Look carefully at the map showing Sicily
and Sardinia and answer the questions.

1   What are the names of the principal
    towns in Sicily?

2   Is Cagliari north or south of Naples?

3   Which island is further west, Sicily
    or Sardinia?

4   Which mountain is shown on the map,
    and how high is it?

5   Naples is about 100 kilometres from
    Rome – true or false?

13 Using fewer words ▶   SB pp114–115

Choose a word from the box to replace the phrases in italics in these sentences.

distinctive   gilded   enthusiastic   hospitable
well-preserved   remote   mosaics

1   The floors of the palace were covered in *lots of coloured bits of stone cut and
    fitted together to make a pattern.*

2   I can recognise Picasso's paintings because his style is so *unusual and different
    from all other artists.*

3   It was such a special occasion that even the cups we drank our coffee from were
    decorated with gold paint around the edges.

4   The Irish family we stayed with were very *kind and welcoming and made sure
    we had everything we could possibly want.*

5   For our holiday we deliberately chose somewhere *far away from other places.*

6   The buildings we saw on our sightseeing tour were old but *care had been taken
    to look after them and keep their original features.*

7   Michael was chosen for the job of tour guide because at the interview he seemed
    so *interested in the work and keen on doing it well.*

14 Sentence correction ▶

Add the missing word in the right place in each of the following sentences.

1   What is the name that island in the Mediterranean?

2   I would have visited you if I known you were coming to this area.

3   We walked for hours and when we stopped we were tired to eat our picnic.

4   Celia is the same weight and size her brother.

5   On holiday, we went to see the house Anne Frank lived.

6   Claude wanted to go to the cinema but we preferred go to a cafe.

7   If he doesn't hurry up, the train leave without him.

15 Using adverbs as intensifiers ▶ SB p116

Complete each sentence with a suitable phrase from the box. There is one more than you need.

> hardly recognizable   frantically busy   dazzlingly bright
> exceptionally interesting   bitterly cold   heavily in debt
> intricately embroidered   acutely painful   historically accurate
> completely exhausted   mentally tiring

1   Before I went to the dentist my bad tooth was _____ .

2   I have always liked Anita Desai's novels but her latest is _____ .

3   I was _____ last weekend trying to finish all my coursework in geography and biology.

4   The midday sun shining on the sea was _____ .

5   Meg lost so much weight during her illness that she was _____ .

6   The children put on warm coats, hats and scarves before going out, as the weather had turned _____ .

7   After a long day spent hiking and climbing, they were all _____ .

8   I enjoy watching films about the kings and queens who lived long ago, but I am not sure that they are always _____ .

9   After losing his money in an unsuccessful business venture, Bernard was _____ .

10 Jordi's work as a computer programmer is not physically demanding but it is _____ .

16 Developing a more mature style ▶ SB p117

Rewrite this description of a holiday destination, Paradise Island, to make it more interesting. Try to use a more mature and sophisticated style.

Paradise Island is shaped like a diamond. It has a lot of rocks on the coastline. The sea is clean. You can see fish in the sea. The beach is white. There are many shells on the beach. There are palm trees along the beach. There are many flowers. You can smell the flowers in the air. There are many birds. The birds sing a lot. The sunsets are good. The sky looks pink. At night there are many stars. There are no tower blocks. There is no traffic. There are no crowds. It is peaceful.

17 Vocabulary building ▶

Mark the odd word out with a ✗ and tick the word which best groups the other words. The first one has been done for you.

1   Zambia Botswana ✗Nepal ✓Africa Namibia Kenya Zimbabwe

2   cottage villa cathedral apartment dwelling farmhouse

3   emerald sapphire diamond ruby jewel pearl valuable

4   hotel resort tourism guide colony sightseeing souvenir

5   gleam glow shine drizzle twinkle sparkle glitter

6   hail rain gale frost fog weather surf

18 Grammar: Adjective plus infinitive ▶

The adjective and infinitive construction is often used to express opinion.
Examples: It is *hard to find* a better quality resort. It is *easy to forget* that Sicily was once the most fought-over island in the Mediterranean.

Choose the best phrase to fill each gap in this text about a student's career plans. There is one more than you need.

awful to live in	pleasing to look at	difficult to know
hard to believe	easy to maintain	expensive to heat
marvellous to visit	idealistic of me to think	

The ancient Egyptians, famous for their pyramids, are said to have been the first architects.
It's (1) _____ that they were able to build the pyramids without

modern aids. It would be (2) _____ Egypt and see for myself the way

they were built. My dream for the future, however, is to work designing houses. So many

modern homes are (3) _____ because they are badly designed and

constructed and require constant repairs. In addition, they often have ill-fitting doors and

windows, which makes them (4) _____ in cold weather. Maybe it's

(5) _____ that I could design the perfect home, but if I become an

architect, I'd like to design practical buildings which are (6) _____ and,

because I think beauty is important, (7) _____ as well.

Now write four sentences of your own, choosing from the following phrases.

exciting to watch   impossible to describe   hard to accept

difficult to cope with   welcome to visit   lucky to win

nice to talk   wrong of him to shout   kind of you to take

careful not to drop   clever of him to pass   delighted to hear

1 _____

2 _____

3 _____

4 _____

19 Compound nouns with *snow* and *sun* ▶

Complete the compound nouns by writing either *snow* or *sun* in each space.

_____shine	_____storm	_____burn	_____light
_____hat	_____ball	_____roof	_____screen
_____flake	_____stroke	_____plough	_____bathe
_____drift	_____dress	_____board	_____tan

20 Spelling revision ▶   SB p119

Make adjectives by adding –y to the words in brackets to fill the gaps. Remember to make any other necessary spelling changes.

1 Plants grow quickly in the warm, _____ air of the rainforest. (steam)

2 Oppressive, _____ weather is more common in the summer. (thunder)

3 We felt seasick as our boat bobbed up and down on the rough, _____ water. (chop)

4 _____ , polluted air blocked out the sunlight. (smoke)

5 Daphne noticed that the white _____ clouds had darkened and it looked as though it would rain. (fluff)

6 When the sun shines through thin, _____ cloud, a coloured ring like a halo may appear. (ice)

7 It was too _____ and _____ to even think of going for a walk. (wind, rain)

21 Text correction ▶

Aidan wrote about a recent school trip for his school newsletter. There are 14 mistakes in his article. Can you find them and correct them?

Lots of tourists are visiting our town each year, but have you ever thought of taking part in some tourist activitys yourself? That's just what we, Year 11, did last week. We took a tourist bus through the centre and saw all kinds of places. I took photographs of the cathedral and of the old monuments in the main square.

After we eaten our packed lunch in Astley Gardens, we visited the Castle Museum. We were taken around by a friendly guide who advised us not to try to see anything but to concentrate on just a few things. He also explained us that many museums now use modern technology to do the exhibits more interesting. For example, he show us how to use computers to investigate ideas of what the town looked like in different historical periods.

After our guided tour, Mr Barnes let us to choose any object in the museum and sketch it. I choosed a strikingly beautiful carved door which had caught my eye earlier. After we had finish sketching we went again outside and were climbing 100 steps to the top of the look-out tower. From such a high point, we had fantastic views over the surrounding area. This was the most good part of the trip for me.

If you want to see our town through new eyes, why not take the tourist bus or visit the museum? You're going to be surprised at what you discover!

UNIT 7 Student Life

SB pp127–132

1 Challenges of student life ▶

What are these students talking about? Match each comment with the correct explanation. There are two more than you need.

1 Can you believe it? My new red shirt has run. Everything is bright pink – even my football shorts!

2 I paid it in yesterday but it will take a few days to be credited to my account.

3 I don't know how, but I must have written down the wrong day. I've had to make another one for next Tuesday.

4 He said the spots hadn't cleared up because I hadn't completed the course.

5 I telephone every Sunday evening to let them know how I'm getting on.

6 I can't go on the picnic. The deadline for my history assignment is Monday, so I'm working all Sunday. Everyone will be out so I'll get a bit of peace and quiet.

7 The rent's not too bad but I've got bills and bus fares on top of that. I have to be careful not to make impulsive buys..

8 It gets really hot, so you have to be careful not to scorch things.

9 The bathroom and kitchen are done on a weekly rota with my flatmates and we do our bedrooms ourselves.

10 I hate tinned stuff, so I pop down to the market at the end of the day. You can get fresh fruit and vegetables cheaper then.

a A cheque
b Ironing clothes
c Eating well
d A missed appointment
e Arrangements to go out for a meal
f Organising time and working alone
g Managing on a budget
h The laundry
i Keeping the house clean and tidy
j A skin problem
k Keeping in touch with the family
l Making new friends

2 Vocabulary check ▶

Decide whether the following sentences are true or false. Give each one a ✔ or a ✗.

1 A *tutorial* may have a lot of students attending at the same time, but you'll only ever find a small number at a *lecture*.

2 A *chore* is a boring kind of job you do in the house, like washing the floor.

3 Payment from the government to help towards studying is called a *grant*.

4 An *essay*, like a composition, is a piece of written work.

5 Missing essay *deadlines* is not important because you can catch up later.

6 An *assignment* is work that is usually done outside class.

7 If you enjoy trying something new, even if you are not sure you will be successful, you like *challenges*.

8   *Coursework* doesn't count towards the final exam marks.

9   A *revision* timetable reminds you when your exams will take place.

10   The marks from a *mock exam* are part of the marks given for the real exam.

3   Compound nouns ▶

Fill each gap with a word from the box to make a common compound noun.

liner   cover   basket   gloves   board   table   pan   case   machine

1   Ramesh made coffee for all the students and put the mugs down on the coffee
_____ .

2   I changed the bed linen and put on clean sheets and pillow_____ .

3   If you want to fry eggs, you'll find a frying _____ in the big kitchen
cupboard.

4   Natalie set up the ironing _____ and started ironing a silk blouse.

5   Don't take a hot dish out of the oven without protecting your hands with oven
_____ , will you?

6   I emptied the rubbish and put in a clean bin _____ .

7   He took the clothes out of the washing _____ and put them in the
laundry _____ .

8   Do you like the pattern on my new duvet _____ ?

4   Prepositions ▶

Complete each sentence with the correct preposition.

1   Luckily, I'm not impulsive _____ shops, or I would spend far too much.

2   I'm not nervous _____ leaving home to get a flat of my own.

3   Can you cope _____ taking care of yourself and studying?

4   Tanya has to manage _____ a tight budget.

5   Have you been in touch _____ your mother since you started university?

6   I can't be with people all the time – I need some time _____ myself.

7   Don't worry about making me dinner. I'll cook _____ myself.

8   Do you enjoy shopping _____ food?

9   It's said a good conversation is similar _____ a ping-pong game.

5   Problems and advice ▶   SB pp130–131

Read each short text and choose the best way of completing it.

1   I was sorry to hear in your letter that you're finding it difficult to keep up with
some of the lectures. I had the same problem at university at first because I wasn't
used to having to listen and take notes at the same time. _____
trying to prepare for your lectures the night before by studying some of the
subject vocabulary you might hear?

   a   It's a good idea to   c   You really have to
   b   Have you ever thought of   d   You could always

2 So you're not sure what topic to choose for your art project work? Why not choose one you're interested in and already know something about? _____ do a project on the history of fashion. You've always been fascinated by the way fashions have changed over time.

    a How about   **c** You'd better
    b You must   **d** You could

3 My landlord is selling the house I live in and he's asked us to leave next month. It's so hard for students to get accommodation here that I was really worried about it and I _____ . But luckily a friend is going to let me share her room until the end of term.

    a didn't know where to turn   **c** had really got a dilemma
    b was grateful for any advice   **d** needed an acceptable solution

4 We had to hand in our coursework yesterday and I was just leaving for college when I realised the folder wasn't in my rucksack. I looked absolutely everywhere but couldn't find it. I was _____ until Anna phoned and said I'd left it round at her place.

    a in need of some advice about this   **c** at my wits' end
    b extremely grateful for any suggestions   **d** considering various possibilities

6 Developing a more mature style ▶   SB p131

Read this letter of reply to a party invitation. Try to rewrite it to improve the tone and register. Use paragraphing where necessary.

Dear Hilary,

I always need a good social scene and I'm afraid I won't be coming to your party. I've been invited to a big disco Barry is giving to celebrate the end of term. It's going to be fantastic and he's taking over the whole of the University Social Centre. Maybe you could check the University Calendar before making plans? It's the best way of avoiding such tragic errors. The point is, you need people to make a party go with a swing and when I think of all the people going to Barry's party, I'm out of my mind with worry for you. So you've managed to persuade your parents to go out for the evening? You may not like lifting a finger, but you should put away ornaments and take up loose rugs before your guests arrive. Your mother will never speak to you again if one of those glass animals she collects gets broken. Here's a little tip I'd like to pass on. Bad music kills a party atmosphere. Do try to choose some decent CDs, as I know what your taste is like. Just put a popular track on loudly as soon as you hear the doorbell. I was glad to hear that your parents have given you some money towards new clothes for your birthday, as it's a shame that you are always so out of fashion. How about spending it at the new boutique in town? It's a great place to shop when you have money to burn. Have a brilliant party and I pray your guests turn up.

Lots of love,

Samira

7 Choose the odd one out ▶

Which of these expressions is not associated with unhappiness from having too much to do?

    a stressed out   **d** rushed off my feet   **f** all tensed up

    b under pressure   **e** at a loose end   **g** snowed under

    c feeling the strain

8 Confusing words ▶

Choose the correct word from each pair in italics.

1 I carry my *diary/calendar* around with me in my bag so I can write down my appointments.

2 I'm *bored/boring* staying at home every night with nothing to do.

3 Rafael is going to have to *rewrite/resit* his exams in the autumn.

4 I asked the *bookkeeper/librarian* to reserve a book on wild flowers for my nature project.

5 The university buildings were a most *impressive/impressing* sight.

6 I like this *exercise/text* book as it covers all the information I need for my course and has lots of good illustrations as well.

7 Combining an active *sociable/social* life with the demands of studying can be a challenge.

8 Borrowing another student's notes is not as good as going to a *conference/ lecture* yourself.

9 In my first year at university I'm going to be living on *campus/camp*.

9 Sentence correction ▶

Add the missing word in the right place in each of these sentences.

1 Emma was pleased not to be dependent her parents.

2 I meant write you last week but I have been so busy doing coursework.

3 I can't believe that only a few weeks ago I living at home with my family.

4 They live in a lovely flat, right the sea.

5 In two years' time Pilar will eighteen and old enough to leave home.

6 We got to the party late and our friends already left.

7 I was so busy revising, I didn't have minute to spare.

8 Mahmoud is studying engineering at a university in USA.

10 Talking about exam pressure ▶ SB pp132–133

Match the halves to make complete sentences. There is one extra 'second half'.

1 It was so nerve-wracking waiting my turn for the oral exam, ...

2 I wanted to work in a restaurant in the evenings but ...

3 You still need to have fun ...

4 I'd been revising all day on my own in the library, so ...

5 It's very difficult to get down to studying if ...

6 One thing I never do after an exam is ...

7 If I'm suffering from exam tension, ...

8 Lin and I hate studying alone, ...

9 Sometimes I leave my books and papers all over the house, but luckily ...

10 My father has laid down the law about ...

a I just had to meet my friends and have some fun.

b even when you're under exam pressure.

c compare answers with my friends.

d you've lost your motivation.

e I went out for a coffee as a way of distracting myself.

f which was a way of using spare time constructively.

g doing my homework before I go out in the evening.

h my mum and dad don't moan about it.

i I go for a long, hard workout at the gym.

j so we meet round at a friend's house and work together.

k my parents put their foot down about it.

11 Informal expressions ▶   SB pp132–133

Choose the best expression to complete each sentence.

> stick to   push me   make up   do my best   brainiest
> too much on his mind   nag you   get on

1 My friend Martin must be the _____ boy in the school. He gets 99% in every test.

2 I can't motivate myself to study. I need someone to _____ .

3 Do your parents _____ about doing homework?

4 It's no good making a work plan if you don't _____ it.

5 Stop daydreaming, Penny, and _____ with your work.

6 If I save most of the money I need for a new CD player, my parents say they'll _____ the rest.

7 I tried hard in that exam because I really wanted to _____ .

8 Don't expect David to tell you whether he wants to join the camping trip yet. He's doing exams and has _____ .

12 *Should, ought, need* and *had better* ▶   SB p135

Rewrite the following sentences using the words in brackets.

1 It was wrong of you to forget Mum's birthday. She was expecting you to phone her.

(shouldn't) _____

2 It isn't necessary to buy any milk when you go out. I bought 2 litres this morning.

(needn't) _____

3 It's important that you take warm clothes with you. It's likely to be cold when you get to Scotland.

(had better) _____

4 I regret not going to bed earlier last night.

(should) _____

5 It is unwise to leave your revision to the last minute.

(oughtn't) _____

6 It's a pity you've already booked a taxi. I could have given you a lift home.

(needn't) _____

13 Understanding visual information ▶

Look at the floor plan of a study centre and decide whether each statement is true or false.

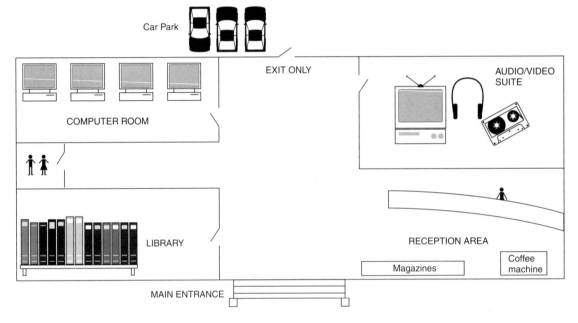

1 The reception area is to the right of the main entrance.

2 There is a coffee machine behind the reception desk.

3 The magazine rack is in the library.

4 The computer room is at the back of the building, on the left.

5 The toilets are near the audio/video suite.

6 There is an exit to the car park.

14 Homophones with silent letters ▶   SB p135

For each of the words below, find a homophone in the box (a word that sounds the same). Write it in the space, then put brackets round the silent letter or letters. The first one has been done for you.

weigh	knight	hour	heir	wrote	which
scent	reign	weight	whether		

1 air _(h)eir_

2 our _____

3 rain _____

4 wait _____

5 night _____

6 witch _____

7 weather _____

8 way _____

9 sent _____

10 rote _____

Now choose three pairs of homophones and write sentences to show their meaning.

1 _____
    _____

2 _____
    _____

3 _____
    _____

15 Capital letters ▶   SB p136

Some of these words need capital letters. Mark all the letters which should be capitals.

mr jones	wednesday	weekend
college	chinese	evening
assignment	september	easter
europe	joseph	india
harvey street	birthday	university of colorado
surgeon	bbc	castle
river nile	himalayas	ramadan
baltic sea	examination	professor grivas

16 Punctuating a text ▶   SB p136

Read this extract from a school report and add any necessary punctuation.

having just marked her last revision test I am concerned that jennifers poor english is

holding her back fortunately she is seeing mr barnes the special needs teacher every

tuesday afternoon for help with grammar spelling vocabulary and handwriting she needs

to make a special effort to improve in these areas

17 Idiomatic expressions ▶   SB p138

Decide whether these sentences make proper sense. Give each one a ✔ or a ✗.

1 Jamal never listened to his parents – their warnings were like water off a duck's back.

2 Catherine joined a course for complete beginners so she was soon out of her depth.

3 Setting her heart on winning the prize led her to give up very easily.

4 Ignacio couldn't make head or tail of the recipe for making soup and phoned his mother to ask for advice.

5 It was pleasant starting a new job and getting the cold shoulder from my new colleagues.

18 Guessing meaning ▶

Guess the meaning of the idiom in italics and write it in the space provided.

'You'll have to *pull your socks up*,' said the headteacher to the student who had received low marks, 'or you'll be leaving this school without a single exam pass.'

Meaning _____

19 Choose the best word ▶   SB p139

Choose the correct word to complete each sentence.

1 A _____ problem among the students is organising their study time effectively.

   a popular   **b** common   **c** several   **d** continuous

2 If you owe money to people, you are in _____ .

   a debt   **b** payment   **c** trouble   **d** debit

3 Despite wanting to pass the exam, Julia just couldn't get down to revising. She seemed to have a mental _____ about it.

   a brick   **b** gap   **c** block   **d** space

4 When the counsellor listened to George's problems, her non-judgmental attitude showed how _____ she was.

   a evaluating   **b** critical   **c** dismissive   **d** supportive

5 Dr Tang's appointment system _____ a set amount of time for each patient.

   a allocates   **b** shares   **c** decides   **d** accepts

6 If you let other people's problems become your problems, you're soon likely to feel _____ .

   a swamped   **b** swept up   **c** suffering   **d** drowned

7 Effective study techniques can make a difference to to how well you _____ information.

   a repeat   **b** remind   **c** remain   **d** retain

8 The file was stamped _____ , so I knew that I shouldn't show its contents to the other people in the office.

   a 'Confidential'   **b** 'Exclusive'   **c** 'Concerning'   **d** 'Attention'

9 Paul gave up buying sweets and magazines for a month. By making these _____ , he managed to save up enough to buy tickets for the concert.

   a denials   **b** pressures   **c** economies   **d** budgets

20 Word formation ▶

Use the words in the box to form new words to complete the passage. The first one has been done for you.

advise   train   knock   appoint   embarrass   occupy   earn

Would you see a college counsellor?

No!

I just don't like the idea of (1) __*knocking*__ on a stranger's door and telling them my problems. Although I visit the doctor occasionally, talking about personal problems with a counsellor would make me feel (2) _____ . I would much rather talk to someone I know and trust, like my best friends or my parents.

Furthermore, I think counsellors could give you bad (3) _____ . They are not like doctors or lawyers who have done a lot of (4) _____ . As I see it, anyone can call themselves a counsellor because it is a relatively new (5) _____ which isn't totally regulated.

Last but not least, a counsellor may ask you to make further (6) _____ when you don't really need to. Perhaps I'm being cynical, but don't forget that the counsellor is (7) _____ money from your visits, so it's in his or her interest to continue seeing you.

Now do the same with the following passage.

discussion	choice	fantasy	positively
confidence	organisation	effective

Would you see a college counsellor?
Yes!

Our college has a (8) _____ counsellor who really understands your problems. There are actually two different ones, and you can (9) _____ which one you prefer to see. You (10) _____ your problems and are helped to see for yourself what would be the best thing to do.

I saw Mrs Hobson once when I was under a lot of exam pressure. She really helped me talk things through and (11) _____ my work better. Talking to her I realised that my father's illness had had a bad (12) _____ on me and that my exam nerves were probably linked to that. My visits to the counsellor were completely (13) _____ , so I felt secure there. Going to a college counsellor is definitely a (14) _____ move, to my mind.

21 Sentence correction ▶

Find the extra word in each of these sentences and cross it out.

1 Before he started on to his biology revision, James went through lots of past papers to identify typical questions.

2 Since the time began, parents have worried about their children's happiness.

3 It's important to find a balance when you are planning your revision timetable and not to do too much or too little of studying at any one time.

4 Fresh air, enough sleep, a healthy diet and some do regular exercise all make a difference to how alert you feel.

5 When students first leave home, they can experience a wide variety of problems and we have a college counsellor is available to help deal with their difficulties.

6 I keep a great collection of humorous videos which are guaranteed to make you laugh at, however stressed out and under pressure you are feeling.

22 Tone and register round-up ▶

Choose the best response to each of the following comments.

1 I couldn't find a pair of socks that would match this morning. I'm wearing two odd ones under these trousers.

   a You must have been out of your mind with worry.
   b At least you found an acceptable solution.
   c Never mind. They don't show with those shoes.
   d I can't bear to be badly dressed either.

2 I was painting my nails for the party when I smudged one, just before I had to go out.

   a It's a shame to see you in such a state.
   b I noticed straightaway they weren't right.
   c You should have started again immediately.
   d That often happens to me too.

3 I was looking after my nephew, who's only three. He was eating an apple when suddenly he started choking. He was gasping for breath but he managed to cough it up after a few seconds.

   a You shouldn't have given him that apple.
   b I expect you needed some advice about that.
   c Oh dear. What an anxiety for you.
   d You really need to go on a first aid course.

4 I think I've put on weight lately. These new trousers feel a bit tight.

   a If I were you, I wouldn't know where to turn.
   b Don't worry. Fat people can look as good as slim ones.
   c Really? I think you look great.
   d No-one around here cares what you look like.

5 My interview for college was pretty scary. I was too nervous to do my best.

   a Have you ever thought of getting help for your nerves?
   b Next time you have an interview, you should prepare properly for it.
   c That's a shame, but you've got other interviews to go to.
   d You must be really heartbroken.

6 I found my history exam today really hard.

   a Get your act together or you won't pass anything.
   b You'll probably get nought per cent.
   c I can't wait to hear your results.
   d You've probably done better than you think.

7 My brother's very upset because his girlfriend has just broken off their engagement.

   a How sad for him.
   b I have to say I'm not surprised.
   c She wasn't a very nice girl, was she?
   d What on earth is he going to do?

8 I was cycling to college this morning when I almost hit a bus coming round the corner. I managed to get out of the way just in time.

   a Phew, that must have been frightening!
   b How about cycling less dangerously in future?
   c What a tragic accident!
   d I'm overwhelmed with relief at your safe arrival.

Happy Endings

---

1 Sea vocabulary ▶ SB p146

Match the definitions with the sea vocabulary. There are two extra words.

1	smooth, round stones	**a**	flotsam and jetsam
2	a plant growing underwater	**b**	current
3	pieces of wood which float on water or are washed onto the beach	**c**	shore
		d	port
4	wood and rubbish from the sea	**e**	seaweed
5	white water made by strong waves	**f**	pebbles
6	water moving in one direction	**g**	driftwood
7	a large passenger ship	**h**	surf
8	the land along the edge of the sea	**i**	dunes
9	a lot of small stones on a beach or by a river	**j**	liner
		k	shingle
10	a town with a harbour, where ships load and unload	**l**	mast

---

2 Vocabulary check ▶ SB p146

Choose the correct word from each pair in italics.

1 Mr Penrose works at the *jetty/docks* unloading *cargo/baggage* from ships that transport goods from all over the world.

2 The captain stood on deck and scanned the *horizon/cliffs* for signs of another ship.

3 We have a small boat and always check the times of high and low *tide/spray* before launching it.

4 I went *snorkelling/windsurfing* on holiday and saw all kinds of fascinating sea life below the surface of the water.

5 The *smugglers/pirates* who brought perfume and cigarettes into the country illegally have just been caught by the police.

6 Eddie is hoping for the right kind of wind when he sails his *dinghy/speedboat*.

---

3 More sea vocabulary ▶ SB p146

Add the missing letters to the incomplete words in these sentences.

1 Sea creatures range in size from enormous w_____s to tiny organisms which can only be seen by a microscope.

2 A s_____r is another name for a captain.

3 There are five _____s in the world and the largest is the Pacific.

4 In the past, people going on a sea v_____ feared fierce bands of p_____s who attacked ships. They stole the ship's c_____o and robbed the passengers.

5 If you see a boat in difficulty, you should immediately contact the co_____, who will organise a rescue.

6 A l_____e flashes a special light to warn s_____s that danger is near.

7 People say that d_____s are intelligent animals who can 'talk' to one another under the water.

8 My little sister loves walking along the beach, collecting s_____s of different shapes and sizes.

9 A v_____l is a word which can be used for any kind of ship.

10 Sailing boats vary in type from small d_____s to large y_____s.

4 Onomatopoeic words ▶   SB p146

Choose the right onomatopoeic word in each sentence.

1 Little Bella loves *squelching/squeaking/squashing* through mud after a rainy day.

2 The children ran into the sea and screamed with delight as they *slipped/sloshed/splashed* each other with cold water.

3 Can you hear the *howling/cracking/flapping* of the wind on a stormy night?

4 The waves *roared/slapped/hooted* against the side of our boat as we sped through the water.

5 The *twittering/screeching/lapping* of the seagulls woke me up on my first day at the seaside.

6 Have you ever tried *smacking/skimming/sliding* stones over the lake?

5 Describing problems and challenges ▶

Match the halves to make complete sentences.

1 We were almost in despair of being rescued when . . .

2 During the round-the-world voyage he longed to receive . . .

3 Silvio suffered all kinds of misfortune, including . . .

4 Spending time with a sick relative has made me appreciate . . .

5 Claudia tries to look on the bright side of things, in spite of . . .

6 Costas lost his hearing and had to live . . .

7 How can anyone resist . . .

8 My sister-in-law has never been contented and is always wishing for . . .

9 Lacking a proper boat to cross the river, they improvised . . .

10 The government's supporters remained loyal despite . . .

a more money and material things.

b losing his job and being hurt in a car crash.

c the call of the sea?

d in a silent world.

e news from his family at home.

f a ship appeared on the horizon.

g a simple raft made from fallen logs.

h her many difficulties.

i the malicious rumours that were being circulated.

j the fact that no amount of money can buy health.

6 Narrative tenses ▶ SB p148

Correct the verb mistakes in these sentences. One sentence has no mistakes.

1 They didn't look thin, considering that they were not eating a proper meal for several weeks.

2 At first, he has been devastated by the shipwreck, but gradually he adjusted to his situation.

3 When we arrived at the harbour, the ferry we going to catch had already left.

4 We sowed lots of green beans in the spring, but only a few came up.

5 Irene was relieved when the boat finally docked as she was feeling seasick for the last two hours.

6 The crew managed to escape from the ship before it has sunk.

7 I was looking on the floor of the cafe for a ring I had lost, when the owner come up and ask if I lost anything.

8 I was skateboarding in the park when I fallen over and hurt my knee badly.

7 Forming questions ▶ SB p149

You are interviewing a couple who survived being adrift at sea for months. Unjumble the sentences to make direct questions. Put a capital letter at the beginning and a question mark at the end.

1 you ever up hope did give

2 longer you think could survived do much how you have

3 big how Ocean Pacific is the

4 good now you are in health

5 preparations you make what journey for did the

6 is how a big whale sperm

7 your plans for future are the what

8 think were about what you while you raft on the did

9 do what taste like sharks

10 you keen are sailing still on

8 Collocations ▶

Cross out the wrong word in each group of four.

1 rough: sea film material surface

2 light: flares air fire matches

3 rescue: dogs children potatoes seagulls

4 waves: crash roar lap screech

5 ships: hoot sink drown sail

6 survive: fire cancer insult shipwreck

9 Ordering events ▶   SB pp150–151

Try to put these sentences into the correct order.

a Before setting off on a trip now, I get my maps out and check the coastline really carefully.

b Initially, I had quite a few problems with the boat, including nearly smashing it up on some rocks and running out of petrol miles from the shore!

c Finally, I inspect the boat to make sure it is seaworthy, and I pack my favourite food and drink for the day.

d After that, if I am still concerned about anything, I'll ring the coastguard to ask for some advice.

e Eventually, after saving for quite a long time, I had enough to buy a second-hand speed boat.

f Then I use the internet to find out the times of the tides and the weather forecast.

g Ever since my parents took me on a boating holiday as a child, I've wanted to have a boat of my own.

h So I started to develop a much more cautious approach.

i So as soon I got my first job, I started saving up all my spare cash.

10 Understanding visual information ▶

Study the following map, which shows a journey made by a group of young people from San Diego. Try to write a short paragraph describing the route they took.

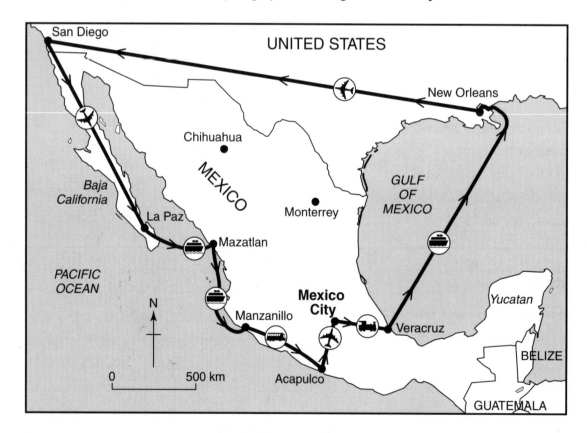

11 Text completion ▶

Read this story from a teenage magazine about a seaside holiday and fill the gaps by adapting the words in brackets.

A happy ending

Have you ever _____ (be) on holiday with your family and really wished you had a friend of your own age around? Last summer my parents and I were _____ (stay) in a caravan on the coast. I loved the area but was feeling a little sad as my best friend, who was supposed to be with me, had _____ (cancel) at the last minute.

One morning I _____ (wake) up very early and decided to collect shells on the beach. The crisp freshness of the early morning air was _____ (delight) after the stuffiness of our holiday caravan. I closed the door behind me as _____ (quiet) as I could, aware of the humped shapes of my parents still fast asleep in their narrow caravan bed.

It was a _____ (glory) morning. The night before, a _____ (violence) storm had blown up, and I had heard huge waves _____ (crash) onto the shore. It is said that in the past many sailors sadly _____ (drown) here, their boats _____ (cruel) smashed on the rocks. This morning, however, the raging energy of the storm had drained away and the air was still and peaceful, like a patient _____ (recover) from a fever which has burned itself out. On the horizon a boat hooted, and above me seagulls _____ (screech) and circled.

The tide was out and the sand was wet and ridged. Eagerly, I rolled up my jeans and _____ (splash) through the cool, shallow water. Now and again a silvery fish slipped across my feet, _____ (remind) me of the underwater world that one day I would love to explore. The sand was studded with shells, and I chose the most interesting-looking ones for my _____ (collect). I bent down and dug out a starfish from the sand, to _____ (inspection) its intricate shape more closely.

The growing warmth of the sun told me that time was _____ (pass). My parents would be waking up and wondering where I was. I was reluctantly turning back when I heard a voice calling me. To my _____ (astonish), I saw my friend Caroline standing on the cliff top and waving. She told me her family's plans had changed and they had _____ (decide) to come to the coast after all.

My brilliant holiday by the sea was now perfect!

12 Vocabulary check ▶   SB pp154–155

Choose the correct word from each pair in italics.

1   The little girl *plummeted/tumbled* down the stairs and had several large, purple *scratches/bruises* on her arms and legs.

2   From the edge of the cliff there is a *sheer/jagged* drop to the rocks below.

3   The children's favourite exercise is *bouncing/pounding* on a trampoline.

4   We were relieved to hear that grandma had survived the operation and that her *condition/state* was stable.

5   Edith came out of the exam feeling very pleased and *convicted/convinced* that she had scored high marks.

6   The twins spend a lot of time playing a game in which they *chase/follow* each other and try not to get caught.

7   After the accident, relatives tried to *condole/console* Asif for the loss of his father.

8   We missed the last train home and were *stranded/strangled* in Paris for the night.

9   When we saw him sitting so *forlornly/hopelessly* in the cafe with the letter in his hand, we knew he had received bad news.

10   The number of casualties was *initially/primarily* reported to be over twenty.

13 Reporting verbs ▶   SB p152

Choose a suitable verb from the box to complete each sentence. Do not use any verb more than once. There is one more than you need.

offered	admitted	estimated	congratulated	threatened	apologised
agreed	explained	complained	boasted	insisted	

1   He _____ that he was more capable than the others who had attempted to sail around the world.

2   After the disaster happened, the purser _____ that she had been at fault for not checking the names on the passenger list.

3   The young yachtswoman was _____ on her outstanding achievement.

4   Our neighbour has _____ to take our children to watch the boat rally.

5   Alex _____ for forgetting to send a telegram saying that he had arrived safely.

6   The authorities _____ that the storm damage would cost around two million dollars to repair.

7   We approached several companies for sponsorship and finally a soft drinks company _____ to donate some money to the project.

8   The survivors of the earthquake _____ that the ordeal had given them great inner strength.

9   The school Principal has _____ on having tornado drills in case of an emergency.

10   The ship's passengers _____ that the cabins were too small and the meals were tasteless.

14 Sentence completion ▶   SB pp154–155

Complete each sentence with the correct preposition or adverb.

1   I admire people who are brave enough to abseil _____ cliffs.

2   Marina is normally late, but she managed to turn _____ on time _____ the celebrations.

3   The ball bounced _____ the pavement into the road.

4   They refused to give _____ hope _____ finding survivors when the building collapsed.

5   We feed our dog _____ tinned dog food and biscuits.

6   There is a good supply _____ fresh lobster _____ the local fishermen.

7   The police are _____ pursuit _____ a gang of smugglers who are bringing contraband goods _____ the country.

8   Before the steam engine was invented, ships had to rely _____ the wind.

9   The children stood _____ silence while their names were called out.

10 Mr Haramis is the officer _____ charge _____ the fire and rescue service.

15 Sentence correction ▶   SB pp154–155

In each of these sentences there is one extra word which shouldn't be there. Find it and cross it out.

1   Losing his beloved pet on a holiday was a traumatic experience which left Luis feeling heartbroken.

2   I'll never forget the seaside cottage in Brittany we rented it a few summers ago for two weeks.

3   On our recent school trip to Scotland, I couldn't find my wallet and I was convinced I must have lost it there on the journey, but when I got home I found it exactly where I had left it - on my bed!

4   The climbers were emaciated and stressed after their ordeal in the mountains but they gradually regained in their health and good spirits.

5   Liz and Martin were distraught when they realised that the train had set off and before they had left their baby behind on the platform.

6   People pamper their pets by giving them treats, too much good food and too little of exercise, but this really isn't a healthy way of life for an animal.

16 Defining relative clauses ▶   SB p156

Write sensible and interesting relative clauses to complete these sentences.

1   On holiday I prefer to visit places where _____
    _____

2   A whale is a mammal which _____

3   'We are hoping for a miracle', said the man whose _____
    _____

4   A tug is small boat that _____

5   The time when _____ was the happiest of Zarina's life.

6   Tsunamis are unusually strong ocean waves which _____
    _____

7   Jacques met the officer who _____

8   Has the coastguard explained what _____ ?

17 Adverb formation ▶   SB p158

Form adverbs from the adjectives in the box to complete these sentences. Be careful with the spelling. The first one has been done for you.

> suitable   joyful   romantic   steady   extraordinary   extreme
> pathetic   simple   immediate   dramatic   responsible

1 When the ship hit an iceberg, the helmsman was _extraordinarily_ brave.

2 We made sure our first aid box was _____ equipped with bandages, antiseptic and plasters.

3 The famous actress's name has been _____ linked with the captain of a large cruise liner.

4 The winds that blow _____ towards the Equator are called *trade winds* because cargo-carrying sailing ships used to rely on them.

5 After months adrift at sea, the couple were _____ thin and weak.

6 The Dead Sea is so full of salt that is said to be _____ difficult to sink in it.

7 Natalie reacted so _____ during the crisis that she was _____ promoted to officer rank.

8 The blueness of the Aegean Sea can be _____ explained by the amount of sunlight reaching the water's surface.

9 The Gulf Stream is a warm ocean current which _____ affects the climate of Northern Europe.

10 'I've just won a place on a training course for navigating officers!' exclaimed Ralph _____ .

18 Obeying the rules of a narrative ▶   SB p161

Remember: a narrative should obey the simple rules of *Who?, What?, Where? Why?, How?* and *When?* In a short story, these are often covered at the beginning.

Read this opening to a story. Mark it ✔ if the rules have been obeyed and ✗ if they have not been followed.

> It was a golden autumn day and Donald and his father were driving towards the naval college on the coast where Donald, who had recently left school, was going to start a marine technology course. Donald had been so excited when his letter of acceptance arrived, but now that they were actually setting off he was feeling rather apprehensive.
>
> They were not far from the college when suddenly a distressed-looking man ran into the road, flagging the car to a halt. Apparently his little boy had climbed onto the roof of their flat to rescue a kitten and was now trapped up there.

19 Text completion ▶

Read this letter describing an eventful day and think of ONE suitable word to fill each gap.

Dear Joanna,

You know how crazy I am (1) _____ photography? Well, something happened recently (2) _____ nearly put an end to my hobby!

Last Sunday I woke up to a bright, breezy morning and, on the spur of the moment, decided to do what I like (3) _____: taking my camera to Formray Island. (I'm sure you remember the uninhabited island we visited together when you came to stay last summer?)

I (4) _____ a ticket for the motor boat that runs weekly (5) _____ to the island. During the short journey I was (6) _____ busy checking my rucksack and scanning the horizon for interesting seabirds to talk to the other (7) _____, who were mostly middle-aged tourists. The boat soon arrived and I (8) _____ ashore.

I (9) _____ a wonderful day wandering over the small island, observing the behaviour of seals and all kinds of birds, including colourful puffins. The strong, clear light was perfect (10) _____ taking photographs, and the salty tang of the sea air brought all my senses alive. I only (11) _____ you could have been there to share it all with me. To my delight, I (12) _____ to get a brilliant photograph of a family of seals. I'll (13) _____ it to you when you next come to visit.

I was happily absorbed watching a baby bird being coaxed to eat by its mother when suddenly I heard the chug-chug of a boat engine. To my (14) _____, I saw the motor boat heading off briskly in the direction of the mainland. Stupidly, I had (15) _____ to check my watch and obviously no-one was aware that I had been left behind! I grew more and (16) _____ panicky as I realised the tide was coming in, and the silence began to seem quite eerie.

I must have been sitting for about an hour feeling increasingly (17) _____ when, amazingly, I heard the sound of another engine. Scanning the shore, I saw a young (18) _____ getting out of a speedboat. I rushed over and told them what had happened, and they kindly offered to take me (19) _____ to the mainland. I was so grateful, I almost hugged them with relief!

As we sped homewards, I turned to catch a glimpse of the island. It looked beautiful in the fading (20) _____ of the day but I was so glad I was leaving, as you can imagine.

Do write soon and tell me all your news.

Love,

Patricia

The Animal World

1 Parts of animals ▶

Fill each space with a word from the box. Some words can be used more than once.

hump	beak	horns	hooves	paws	feathers	mane
tusks	wings	trunk	fur	claws	fins	scales

bird   **cat**   **horse**   **camel**

_____   _____   _____   _____

_____   _____   _____   _____

_____   _____

_____

elephant   **goat**   **fish**

_____   _____   _____

_____   _____   _____

2 Vocabulary check ▶   SB pp165–166

Decide whether the following sentences are true or false. Give each one a ✔ or a ✗.

1 Plants or animals which are alike in some way are a *species*.

2 If an animal hunts and kills you, you have become its *prey*.

3 Animals which hunt and kill live animals for food are *scavengers*.

4 Animals which sleep throughout the winter are *migrating*.

5 When the last animal dies, the species has become *endangered*.

6 Zoo animals which give birth are *breeding in captivity*.

7 Zoo animals which live in secure open spaces are in *enclosures*.

8 Animals which cannot survive outside water are *amphibians*.

9 If you find a trace of a bird or animal preserved in rock, you have found a *fossil*.

10 If an animal is used to living with other animals, it is *domesticated*.

11 Hunting may be legal but *poaching* never is.

12 If an animal is kept in a box with bars, it is in a *cage*.

3 Text completion ▶

Read this history of zoos and fill each gap with the best word from the choices at the end.

A history of zoos

No-one can be certain when zoos first began, but (1) _____ believe the first
'zoo' may have belonged to Queen Hatshepsut in ancient Egypt. Ancient Chinese
emperors are also thought to have collected different types of birds, fish and animals from
all over their (2) _____ . The creatures were kept in pleasant gardens where

they could feel at home. Such places were essentially (3) _____ , and the animals were kept for the pleasure and entertainment of their owners.

Although kings and queens continued to collect animals and exchange exotic creatures as gifts, it was not (4) _____ the 1700s that scientists began to study animals in order to (5) _____ them. Animals were sorted into groups and given Latin names. This meant that the same animal would have the same name wherever (6) _____ lived. The idea of creating a public zoo was a direct (7) _____ of the scientists' work. London Zoo, the first zoo to be opened to the public, was built in 1829.

Our understanding of the needs of animals in captivity has grown since the early days of public zoos. Modern zoos attempt to create natural settings (8) _____ their animals and to provide a reasonable amount of freedom. Wherever possible, fences, hedges and moats are used instead of cages to separate animals (9) _____ visitors. Polar bears and seals have pools to splash in. In specially darkened buildings, people can see animals which are normally only (10) _____ at night.

(11) _____ , many animals find it difficult to breed in zoos. The reasons for this are not yet fully understood, (12) _____ it may be linked to the lack of opportunity to follow normal instincts.

1 botanists historians veterinarians biologists
2 country kingdom empire region
3 personal isolated private inclusive
4 from in until when
5 explain know classify order
6 he she it they
7 following result expectation reward
8 in at for of
9 of from by with
10 active alive there aware
11 Despite Although Furthermore Nevertheless
12 so but anyway while

4 Odd word out ▶   SB p178

Which of these is not a collective noun for a group of animals or birds?

herd swarm foal pack flock shoal

5 Linking ideas ▶   SB p167

Complete these paragraphs correctly by choosing an appropriate expression from the box. There is one more than you need.

> As a result   After weighing up the pros and cons
> Despite   To my mind   Furthermore
> but nothing could be further from the truth

1   The biggest fish in the world is the whale shark. People assume it is a highly dangerous animal, _____ . It is, in fact, completely harmless to humans.

2   Apes share many characteristics with humans. They have the same kind of skeletons, teeth and blood. _____ , humans and apes can catch many similar diseases.

3   Tigers kill and eat all kinds of animals, from monkeys to buffaloes. They are skilful swimmers but are not good at climbing. _____ being poor climbers, however, they are able to reach high places by their ability to spring up to six metres.

4   No-one knows exactly why the dinosaurs became extinct, but scientists think that the world's climate grew colder and they found it impossible to hold their body heat. _____ , they eventually froze to death.

5   We've thought for a while about getting a puppy because the children would love to have a pet to care for. Having had a puppy myself as a child, I know they can be quite destructive at first, and if we do get one it will need careful training. _____ , my husband and I have decided to go ahead with the idea.

6 Medical science ▶   SB pp169–170

Match each definition or sentence with the correct word from the box.

> virus   vitamins   vaccine   hormones   veins   blood   antibiotics
> anaesthetic   laboratory   lungs   asthma   ethical

1   A substance used to make a person immune to a disease.

2   Giving an animal organ to a human being poses this kind of question.

3   These form a single organ inside your chest to enable you to breathe.

4   This fluid nourishes our bodies and removes waste products.

5   Two examples of these are insulin and adrenalin.

6   Tubes that take blood to the heart from various parts of the body.

7   This medical condition causes difficulty in breathing.

8   This prevents pain during an operation.

9   You take these to fight some kinds of infection.

10   These are found in food and are needed for healthy growth.

11   A tiny living particle which causes disease.

12   This is the place where scientists carry out their experiments.

7 Prepositions ▶ SB pp171-172

Complete each sentence with a suitable preposition. Sometimes more than one preposition is possible.

1 The link _____ cancer and smoking has led many people to give up the habit.

2 We're just not happy with the scientists' treatment _____ animals.

3 Animals are obviously different _____ people.

4 This university is famous _____ its research _____ cystic fibrosis.

5 Paola campaigned tirelessly _____ better treatment of animals.

6 We were disgusted _____ the actions of some of the campaigners.

7 Who knows what goes on _____ the closed doors _____ a laboratory?

8 The educational campaign led to dramatic improvements _____ child health.

9 Was Doctor Araj sympathetic _____ your problem?

10 The TV programme was clearly biased _____ animal experiments. The positive aspects were ignored.

8 Understanding graphs ▶

The graph gives information about the use of animals for cosmetics testing in a European country. Decide whether the statements below are true or false.

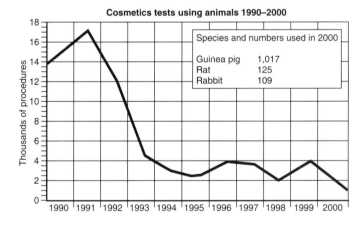

Cosmetics tests using animals 1990–2000

Species and numbers used in 2000

Guinea pig	1,017
Rat	125
Rabbit	109

1 The information spans a period of twelve years.

2 Testing peaked in the middle of 1991.

3 The sharpest fall was between 1991 and 1993.

4 Numbers rose and then fell in 1997.

5 The general trend was downwards.

6 Over a thousand different species of animals were used in the testing.

9 Expressing strong opinions ▶ SB pp174–175

Match the halves to make logical sentences about hunting animals for sport.

1 Rico says shooting baby birds is a harmless fieldsport, but as I see it, …

2 The campaigners protest against cruelty to animals but …

3 Although shooting is just a game to many who take part, …

4 Let's face it, stopping the fox hunt on Saturday …

5 I believe raising people's awareness is the best method of ending …

6 Why should people lose the pleasure of following a traditional sport …

7 People claim that foxhunting helps farmers keep the fox population down, yet …

8 What's worse: the nightmare to farmers of allowing foxes to kill their new-born lambs, …

a just because a few crazy protesters claim it's immoral?

b the abuse of animals in sport.

c isn't going to be easy.

d it is nothing but a wicked bloodsport.

e they are perfectly happy to eat meat.

f is it as much fun for those animals on the receiving end?

g a ban on it would have no significant impact on the numbers in rural areas.

h or killing foxes quickly and cleanly in a well-organised hunting event?

10 Adding adjectives for emphasis ▶ SB p175

Choose an adjective from the box to make each sentence more effective. There is one more than you need.

anxious   preposterous   innocent
enchanting   apologetic   compassionate

1 We were disturbed to hear of _____ animals being killed for fun.

2 I laughed at the _____ idea that domestic pets suffer more stress than animals caged in zoos.

3 We were fascinated by the _____ sight of a mother bird feeding her tiny babies.

4 Desmond sent Susy a(n) _____ letter saying how sorry he was for forgetting their arrangement to meet.

5 By her _____ expression, we knew Tina was worried about something.

11 Odd word out ▶ SB p181

Which of these is not a young bird or animal?

cub foal duckling calf cygnet ewe kid lamb kitten

12 Vocabulary check ▶

SB pp174–175

Choose the correct word from each pair in italics.

1 This is a *human/humane* method of controlling the fox population.

2 The children were afraid to touch the dog until the owner said it was perfectly *innocent/harmless*.

3 'Hamlet' is a beautiful and complex Shakespeare play. I think making a cartoon version will only *debase/abuse* it.

4 They were *distressed/disrupted* to hear of the death of their president.

5 Deborah felt such *contempt/contentment* when she found out that the animals were killed for sport.

6 The poor baby was *deprived/depraved* of his right to care and affection.

7 My neighbour's *savage/wild* dog was destroyed, as it was a danger to everyone in the street.

8 The letter from the animal rights group *appealed/applied* to our better nature.

9 Judith found sitting on the hard chair for a long time very *uneasy/uncomfortable*.

10 The museum can give you a lot of *historical/traditional* information.

13 Sentence correction ▶

Add the missing word in the right place in each of these sentences.

1 Snakes make unusual pets which are not that difficult look after.

2 People have always admired eagles for beauty, strength and swiftness.

3 To reduce the risk of disease, bird feeders and trays be cleaned regularly.

4 Animals often shelter inside bonfires, so remember to check them lighting them.

5 We asked our vet whether the puppy would need operation to mend its broken leg.

6 What we need in this town is an animal sanctuary where injured animals can cared for free of charge.

7 It's lovely having a dog, but it can be difficult to find someone to look after her we go away at weekends.

8 An elephant's trunk can carry logs but is also sensitive enough to pick up peanut from the ground.

14 Verb forms ▶

Each of these sentences has a wrong verb form. Can you find it and correct it?

1 Dinosaurs have become extinct a long time ago.

2 Scientists think that early man was keeping dogs to help with hunting.

3 Lizards are feeding on small insects and plants.

4 He needed to see a doctor because the dog had been biting his hand.

5 Ruben has sold his farm ten years ago.

6 For many years the camel was used for transport, especially in desert regions of the world.

7 Intensive farming methods often criticise for being harmful to the environment.

15 Vocabulary check: Food production ▶   SB p179

Choose the correct word from each pair in italics.

1   I'm afraid the apples and pears in the *vineyard/orchard* aren't ripe enough for picking yet.

2   They keep a wide range of *hens/poultry*, including chickens, ducks, and geese.

3   Local milk, butter and cheese come from the *dairy/beef* herds kept on farms around here.

4   Do you know of any farmers who don't *grow/rear* their animals for profit?

5   Scientists believe BSE in cows was caused by *contaminating/corrupting* the food chain.

6   Food that is produced as naturally as possible is known as *generic/organic*.

7   Hens which live in natural conditions produce eggs described as *free range/ home grown*.

8   The farmers are hoping for dry, fine weather when the time comes to *harvest/ collect* their crops.

9   If they don't use *pesticides/subsidies*, how will they control the insects which eat all the grain?

10   I can't see how *processed/manufactured* food can be as good for you as food which goes straight from the grower to the shop.

16   Text completion ▶

Complete this student's composition by thinking of ONE suitable word to fill each space.

Do the advantages of intensive farming outweigh the disadvantages?
Yes!

In the first place, who wants to go back to the bad old days when food

(1) _____ difficult to grow and likely to (2) _____ contaminated? People couldn't even trust the milk because (3) _____ could carry awful bacteria.

In addition, I love going into bright, clean supermarkets and choosing perfect fruit

(4) _____ I know won't poison me, because all the germs (5) _____ been killed off. I don't want to go into grubby food shops (6) _____ the butchers have blood-stained aprons and (7) _____ there are strange and unpleasant smells.

Furthermore, food these days is also (8) _____ cheaper, which means everyone can afford to eat properly. My grandparents could (9) _____ eat cheese once a week and hardly knew (10) _____ meat tasted like!

Finally, people (11) _____ that farm animals are unfairly treated but it's time we accepted what animals are here for. Animals cannot talk or (12) _____ human emotions. Little children enjoy pretty pictures of woolly lambs frolicking

(13) _____ the fields, but everyone has to grow up. We need to eat and we need safe food which is cheaply produced. Why not thank intensive farming (14) _____ providing that for us?

Now do the same with this composition by another student.

Do the advantages of intensive farming outweigh the disadvantages?
No!

In the first place, we call ourselves a civilised society but our exploitation of animals
(15) _____ absolutely disgraceful. Farm animals are kept (16) _____
appalling and most unnatural conditions just (17) _____ that we can buy cheap
meat, eggs and cheese. Intensive farming has also led (18) _____ food surpluses.
Richer countries have 'butter mountains', for example, (19) _____ people in
poorer countries go hungry. To my mind, this is totally immoral.

In addition, the frantic demands (20) _____ intensive production have resulted
in a disruption to the food chain. We have BSE (21) _____ cattle which can
jump species and is now affecting humans. Scientific interference does not stop
(22) _____ . Supermarket shelves are crammed with highly unnatural, genetically-
modified foods. This can only end in disaster (23) _____ the nation's health.

To sum up, I urge all readers to write (24) _____ their newspaper about animal
welfare issues. I know most people, even if they have strong views, don't usually write to
newspapers, (25) _____ your letter really will make a difference. It IS worth it!

17 Sounds right? ▶

The sounds in these sentences have been mixed up! Can you correct them?

1   The kitten began to *bark* for some milk.
2   The snake *purred* when it saw danger approach.
3   The town hall clock *buzzed* midnight as we left the party.
4   We could hear the hens *hissing* as they ran after their chicks in the farmyard.
5   Our dog always *miaows* when someone rings the doorbell.
6   The cat *giggled* with pleasure as it was being stroked.
7   Just listen to that pack of wolves *roaring* on the hillside!
8   Do you like the sound of frogs *howling*?
9   The bees were *chiming* as they flew among the roses in the sunshine.
10   The children *croaked* all the way through the cartoon.
11   The lioness *clucked* when anyone tried to approach her cubs.

18 Writing in a more mature style ▶

Match these extracts from students' writing with extracts a–j written in a more mature style.

1   It is wrong to kill wild animals to make medicines. These medicines do not make you get better from illnesses even when they take them.

2   This means children who are not born at the moment can't see them to know what they were like when they are born because they won't be there to see them.

3   The people who work in the zoo tried to get them to have babies but they didn't want to have babies in the zoo, but they would have them if they were back in their homes.

4   These big animals were in these kind of like cage things and I saw that these great big animals were not happy when they were in there.

5   I stroked this cat's fur and I mean it was a very young baby cat. It felt soft and kind of just like baby fur.

6   There are some animals in Africa and India and I think in places like China and there are not many of them left, and I think they won't be seen in the world much longer.

7   If you give some money now it's going to help and you don't need to give a lot to save them because all the money you give we are going to send to them.

8   Blood-sport is not really like that bad a sport like everyone says and we should worry instead about helping children who haven't got enough money for the hospital.

9   Some people get puppies and pets like that for their birthday and then they don't want them so they just throw them away, and this place has people who find them in the street and they are so good to these poor little animals.

10 I didn't like what he did and it made me feel so bad when I thought about it that I never wanted to think about it again.

a   Some animals dislike breeding in captivity.

b   The kitten's soft, velvety fluffiness was a delight to touch.

c   Why should noble creatures be sacrificed to make useless potions?

d   It's horrifying to think that future generations may never know the splendour of these magnificent beasts.

e   Can we even guess at the suffering of a huge beast trapped in a tiny space?

f   Donating even a few pounds makes a significant difference to the charity's life-saving efforts.

g   Why all the fuss about hunting when children are suffering terribly through lack of basic medical care?

h   The rescue workers at the centre for injured and abandoned animals are most tender towards them.

i   I was sickened by his appalling behaviour.

j   Many endangered species are on the brink of extinction.

The World of Work

1 Who does what? ▶

SB p187

Complete each definition with the correct word from the box.

tycoon	novelist	nursery teacher	miner	cellist	journalist
plumber	labourer	dentist	carpenter	midwife	linguist
firefighter	interior designer	chauffeur	choreographer

1 A(n) _____ takes care of your teeth.

2 A(n) _____ writes novels.

3 A(n) _____ works with languages.

4 A(n) _____ designs the insides of houses.

5 A(n) _____ puts out fires.

6 A(n) _____ writes for a newspaper.

7 A(n) _____ plays a musical instrument.

8 A(n) _____ owns a large and successful business.

9 A(n) _____ works with very young children.

10 A(n) _____ does physical work repairing roads etc.

11 A(n) _____ makes things out of wood.

12 A(n) _____ extracts coal or metals from under the ground.

13 A(n) _____ is employed to drive a car for a rich person.

14 A(n) _____ delivers babies.

15 A(n) _____ repairs water pipes etc.

16 A(n) _____ designs dances for the stage.

Now think of three more occupations and write their definitions.

1 _____

2 _____

3 _____

2 Word formation: Feelings and abilities ▶

Change each word in italics into the correct form, to fit the meaning of the sentence.

1 Helena was very *disappoint* not to be given the job.

2 It was *frustration* not to be able to video my favourite programme.

3 Jeremy took the toy engine apart because he was *intrigue* about the way it worked.

4 Her *enthusiastic* for the work of the department really impressed the interviewers.

5 Mr Biswan refused to become *despond* when his business went through difficult times.

6 The marketing team were *elate* when their advertising campaign succeeded.

7 Manolo's *determine* and *initiate* make him an asset to any department.

8 Thinking up new ideas required *creation*.

9 His self-*disciplinary* was very strong and he had no difficulty finishing the project on his own.

10 Cristina's *patience* nature was an asset when she began working with children with learning difficulties.

11 I don't have the necessary *dexterous* to sew my own clothes.

12 My uncle showed great *courageous* when the doctors told him the disease was incurable.

13 A powerful *imagine* is essential for a novelist.

14 I admire Dominic's *persevere*. He won't give up, however difficult the task.

3 Vocabulary check ▶   SB pp188–191

Choose the correct word from the box to complete each sentence. Make sure you use each word only once.

| launch | investing | profitable | brand | formula | products | research |
| packaging | campaign | manufacturing | competitive | consumers |

1 They decided to carry out further market _____ to assess whether the new idea was likely to succeed.

2 I love the unusual blue and gold _____ of those luxury biscuits.

3 The company didn't go ahead with the new kind of drinking chocolate because they couldn't get the _____ right.

4 It's difficult to make money in his business because it's a very _____ market.

5 They want to increase production and are _____ in a new factory.

6 The company had to close down because it wasn't _____ .

7 Apparently, _____ are spending proportionately more on clothes and less on food these days.

8 We plan to _____ our new range of swimwear in April.

9 The directors met to plan their advertising _____ for the following year.

10 Did you realise that only one in ten new _____ are successful?

11 Have you tried this new _____ of coffee? It's really delicious.

12 The cosmetics company gave up the idea of _____ a new kind of lipstick.

4 Choose the best word ▶   SB pp188–189

Choose the correct word to complete each sentence.

1 Karin spilled her drink over her sandwich, making it _____ .

   a soft   **b** soggy   **c** soppy   **d** sagging

2 If you don't get the right _____ of ingredients, the cake won't taste right.

   a balance   **b** percentage   **c** share   **d** division

3   The company bought television _____ to advertise its product.

   a airmiles   **b** airtime   **c** airspace   **d** airwaves

4   Gary not only works hard, but he is also able to _____ a high level of concentration throughout a project.

   a support   **b** sustain   **c** release   **d** gain

5   There is no evidence that the advertisement made any _____ on sales.

   a impact   **b** press   **c** difference   **d** force

6   Don't you think they were wrong to _____ the kitten in the street when they didn't want it any longer?

   a drop   **b** remove   **c** abandon   **d** force

7   The children watched closely while their mother cut the pie into equal

   _____ .

   a rations   **b** divisions   **c** fractions   **d** portions

8   Tomas hoped to marry Josephine and was very disappointed to find out he had a(n) _____ for her affections.

   a equal   **b** partner   **c** rival   **d** opponent

9   We don't think that slightly increasing the prices of our luxury cars will cause a drop in sales. It's not a price- _____ market.

   a sensory   **b** sensitive   **c** sensible   **d** sentient

10 Heidi's job involves inputting _____ about sales patterns into a computer.

   a measures   **b** deals   **c** rates   **d** data

5 Sentence correction ▶

In each of these sentences there is one extra word which shouldn't be there. Find it and cross it out.

1   Companies constantly try to develop the new and different products in order to extend their share of the market and to keep their image fresh.

2   Market research teams are used to investigate in possibilities for new products. They hope to discover new ways of approaching the consumer or meeting it a previously untapped need.

3   Many food manufacturers, for example, have developed as low-fat and low-sugar alternatives to their standard brands to appeal to health-conscious consumers.

4   The growth in vegetarianism has led to the mass production of vegetarian ready-to-eat meals which were unheard of a few of decades ago.

5   I found it surprising to learn that ninety per cent of a new products fail.

6 Approximations ▶   SB pp192–193

Do these approximations make proper sense? Give each sentence either a ✔ or a ✗.

1   The company were worried when the majority of people interviewed, almost 20%, could not remember seeing their adverts on TV.

2   Very few students, about four out of five in the survey, expect to get a job immediately after graduating.

3 About 5% of students, one in twenty, say the long-term prospects are more important when choosing their career than the starting salary.

4 Nearly a third (63%) were satisfied with the careers counselling they had received.

5 Getting on for a half (49%) of respondents gave convenience to home as a reason for choosing their present employment.

6 We were very surprised when we read that nearly a quarter of local residents (14%) had complained about teenagers making noise at night.

7 Questioning information ▶   SB p192

Match the halves to make complete sentences. There is one extra 'second half'.

1 The government investigation pleased everyone as it finally ...

2 The director didn't have time to read through the whole report, so he asked his assistant ...

3 We were angry when the politicians said that teenagers are happy to be out of work as we think this only ...

4 Local people feel annoyed about the closure of the clinic and a public meeting has been called so that they can ...

5 We were furious when we read the article claiming that young people are to blame for the problems in the community. It's a total ...

6 The bus company's report is fudging the facts when it claims a high level of satisfaction with the bus service. Everyone ...

7 It's ridiculous to say that no limit should be set on working hours. Who on earth ...

8 The factory owner was accused of bending the truth when he claimed that the workers had refused ...

9 We didn't take the results of the survey seriously as ...

10 The report which claims that doctors in poorer districts are not as good as those who work in affluent places is misleading because it's ...

11 Would you trust a report from a confectionery manufacturer claiming ...

a air their grievances.

b chocolate is not really harmful to children's teeth?

c distortion of the truth.

d exposed the facts about water contamination in the town.

e clouds the real issues.

f I know thinks it's terrible.

g to take paid holidays.

h to highlight the main points for him.

i dreamed that idea up?

j the size of the sample was so small.

k twisted the results.

l not comparing like with like.

8 A training scheme for young people ▶   SB pp192–193

Using the prompts, build up a report describing a training scheme for young people.

New training scheme/offer high-quality training/school and college leavers/aged 16 and upwards/the employer's premises/wide range/occupations. Some employers be initially reluctant/take part/and say/they be worried/teenagers be/bad employment risk. However, their fears be/proved groundless/and they now say/media image/young people/be total distortion/truth.

Scheme give/training opportunities/engineering/hairdressing/manufacturing/and show/teenagers be hardworking/enthusiastic/reliable and quick/learn. Employers themselves design/scheme/so it be genuinely useful/them. 76%/local employers/recruit teenagers/scheme/and next year/it be hoped/area/reach/government target/85%. Employers say/two out of three youngsters make/'better progress than expected'/and there be/drop-out rate/less than ten per cent.

Recent government report conclude/experience be invaluable/those/take part. Four-fifth trainees/scheme/say it be/only way/earn and learn/same time. Most be very impressed/scheme/and plan/recommend it/their friends.

9 Comparing information in charts ▶

Study the bar charts and correct any information which is wrong in the following sentences.

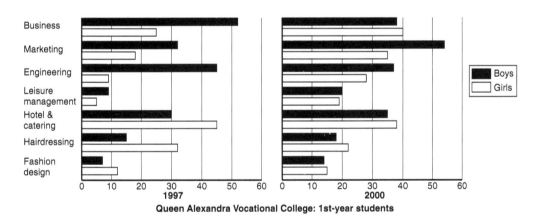

Queen Alexandra Vocational College: 1st-year students

1 The most popular choice for girls in 1997 was hotel and catering, whereas for boys it was the business course.

2 The year 2000 saw a dramatic rise in the number of girls studying engineering.

3 The least popular course overall in 2000 was hairdressing.

4 The number of girls studying marketing almost doubled between 1997 and 2000.

5 More girls than boys chose the business course in 2000.

6 Business grew in popularity with both boys and girls.

10 Employment vocabulary ▶   SB p195

Choose the correct word from the box to complete each sentence. There is one more than you need.

> promoted   clinched   sack   realistic   staffing   knowledge
> recruit   disciplinary   displayed   attributes   targets

1   Until the contract for new business was actually signed, the company did not feel it had _____ the deal.

2   The taxi company has increased _____ levels this year and has taken on four new drivers.

3   The Bestbuy sales assistant was extremely helpful, and his extensive product _____ meant he could give us excellent advice about which camera would be best for our needs.

4   After only six months in the job, Lu's enthusiasm and ability led her to be _____ to store manager.

5   As the store is situated in an area of declining population, hoping to double the sales of electronic goods in the next six months just isn't _____ .

6   If Keith keeps being late for work, his manager is going to take _____ action.

7   We employ people from many different backgrounds. What matters most is whether they have the skills and _____ needed for the job.

8   If sales go on increasing, we will need to _____ more staff.

9   The electrical department is very big, but the goods are so well _____ it was easy to find the type of microwave I was looking for.

10   Two members of staff got the _____ recently for stealing from the office.

11 Punctuating a text ▶

Add the punctuation and paragraphing to this text about personnel work.

jan benson is employed as an assistant to a personnel officer for a big clothing chain in scotland personnel is often stereotyped as lacking in excitement says jan but the work can offer a fulfilling career to anyone who has a genuine desire to make organisations more efficient jan took a degree in economics at birmingham university before deciding she was interested in personnel work I started as an assistant to a personnel officer last august and have been studying for my qualifications in personnel management in the evenings explains jan its hard work but worth it as im able to go on earning while im gaining qualifications the aspect jan most enjoys about her work is the challenge of gaining the respect of the store managers im learning from my boss mrs harris that its essential to try to be in tune with the needs of the managers rather than just imposing my views on them she explains

12 Odd word out ▶

Which of these is the odd word out? Why?

supporting   caring   pitying   loving   despising   empathising   sympathising

13 Guessing meaning from context ▶

Try to guess the meaning of the words and phrases in italics.

1 Sales continued to fall until the company *went bust*.

2 The farmer decided to *diversify*, so as well as keeping cattle he offers holiday accommodation to tourists.

3 The factory sells directly to the consumer and by cutting out the *middleman* they keep prices down.

4 It was difficult to run the business on his own, so he went *into partnership*.

14 Vocabulary check ▶   SB p197

Decide whether the following sentences make proper sense and give each one either a ✔ or a ✗. Think carefully about the meanings of the words in italics.

1 The dog was so *pampered* that its owners never bothered to take it to the vet when it was ill.

2 Simon has a very *tactful* manner and often hurts people's feelings unintentionally.

3 Louisa couldn't afford a new dress, but she took care to wash and iron the outfit she was wearing to the job interview so that she would look *presentable*.

4 *Hearing impairment* can be a great asset when choosing to train as an interpreter.

5 Sign language helps to break down the *language barrier*.

6 I need to learn Japanese quickly, so a *crash course* wouldn't be any use.

7 Hamida was worried when she found that the new job provided a *supportive* environment.

8 I was *spoiled* as a child because my parents were very strict with me and we had lots of rules at home.

9 I was lucky when I went on work experience because I had a very kind *mentor* who guided me through the job.

10 Juan is so *agile* that he even finds it difficult to bend down far enough to put his shoes on.

15 Choose the best word ▶   SB p197

Choose the correct word or phrase from each pair in italics.

1 I had never used a computer and felt *at a loss/at risk* when I was asked to use one in my new job.

2 Professor Rashid's research into hearing problems is seen by scientists as *groundbreaking/backbreaking* work.

3 Paul felt *left out/on his own* when he realised he was the only applicant who had not been selected for work experience.

4 The restaurant was not sure if customers would like the new pasta dishes so they started *cautiously/curiously* by offering only one new dish at a time.

5 When the police stopped Wendy for speeding, she was *released/relieved* to be given just a warning.

16 Phrasal verbs with *up*, *down* and *out* ▶   SB pp198–199

Complete each sentence with a phrasal verb from the box. Do not use any verb more than once.

> drew up   let down   turned down
> put him down   drew out   jotted down   turned up

1 Anna's application was _____, as she was too young for the training scheme.

2 When none of his friends offered to help him, Ben felt very _____ .

3 I _____ the telephone number on a scrap of paper.

4 We _____ a list of all the things we wanted to achieve in our new business.

5 Ali was younger and smaller than everyone else in the group but no-one ever _____ .

6 The manager's skilful leadership _____ the best qualities in her staff.

7 Leah finally _____ when her friend had been waiting over half an hour.

17 Sentence correction ▶

Add the missing word in the right place in each of these sentences.

1 I spent time the workplace observing my mentor carrying out her duties.

2 Although he was a very strict boss, he was most loving his wife and children.

3 The grass on the lawn was so smooth and thick it looked a green carpet.

4 I couldn't speak to the personnel manager as he gone to lunch.

5 I've always wondered what it would be like to a cook in a busy restaurant.

6 You'd better keep an eye on the milk in the saucepan it could boil over.

7 The steep steps made the premises inaccessible disabled people.

8 What sort of career you decided to follow?

9 The company will pay you money you study for vocational qualifications.

18 Collocations ▶

From each group below, cross out the noun which cannot follow the adjective.

1 regular: supporter player brother party-goer

2 reliable: minibus smile worker service

3 mixed: person results feelings school

4 strong: candidate coffee ocean friendship

5 senior: prefect doctor teacher mother

6 mature: style thought personality newspaper

19 Sentence construction ▶

Add ONE suitable word to complete each of these sentences.

1 My sister is always saying _____ hard-working she is.

2 He was the one _____ made the most progress.

3 David is not as enthusiastic about football _____ the rest of the team.

4 We've now got an after-school club every Tuesday, _____ has made a real difference to our lives.

5 We had all voted for Maria and wanted to know _____ she hadn't been chosen as team leader.

6 Amy, _____ has been helping at the children's hospital for a few months, has just been made head prefect.

7 Sebastian has decided to learn a foreign language, _____ will be a great advantage to him in his future career.

8 She doesn't like to be interrupted _____ she is working on her project.

9 The fact _____ more students are doing information technology at school shows the importance of it to their future plans.

20 Text completion ▶

Read this text, which gives advice to young people considering their future careers, and fill each space with ONE suitable word.

When you are choosing a future career, good careers advice (1) _____ essential. An expert careers advisor is trained both to (2) _____ you information and to assess your suitability for careers that appeal (3) _____ you.

Being friendly, responsible, honest and punctual (4) _____ useful qualities in most careers. Achievements at school in sport, as a prefect, or helping to organise school trips, or experience outside school (5) _____ as doing voluntary work in the community, will be regarded positively by the careers advisor. It will also provide him or her with valuable (6) _____ about your interests and personal qualities. He or she will also want to know your predicted exam grades, (7) _____ your results are not yet known.

When offering information about a particular career, the careers advisor will want to (8) _____ your level of knowledge of that career. For example, many students say they want a job in 'engineering'. Engineering is (9) _____ enormously broad field, covering a wide range of different occupations, so you will be helped to narrow down the choice and come (10) _____ a better understanding of specific kinds of work. A careers advisor can also be useful when you (11) _____ decided you want a job, say, outdoors, but again have little idea (12) _____ the type of work you could do. He or she will (13) _____ you explore the options and consider related careers, from agriculture (14) _____ leisure management.

Career progression is a further important aspect that the careers advisor will be able to explain, so that you can consider the type of position you (15) _____ hold (16) _____ ten years' time and what you might have to do to get there.

If you visit a college to enquire about courses (17) _____ interest you, be prepared to ask some questions of your own. Probing questions concerning (18) _____ many graduates of a course (19) _____ employment in their field after qualifying are vital.

Other ways of gaining insight into the world of work (20) _____ work experience placements and the opportunity to take (21) _____ in mentoring schemes. College courses often offer these elements as part (22) _____ their vocational training.

21 Colloquial language round-up ▶

Decide whether these sentences make proper sense and give each one either a ✔ or a X. Think carefully about the meanings of the expressions in italics.

1 You take a lot of rest if you *work around the clock*.

2 You're ignoring a problem when you *turn a blind eye* to it.

3 Being the office *dogsbody* is rewarding, well-paid work.

4 You're dissatisfied when you say you're *stuck at home* all day.

5 You're telling the truth when you're *fudging the facts*.

6 The senior nurse got *ruffled feathers* when the health inspector told her to improve her work.

7 *Top-of-the-range* brands of coffee are usually the least expensive.

8 There are too many people giving you orders if you are *your own boss*.

9 When people disagree, they are *not seeing eye to eye*.

10 You'd be surprised if a linguist had *an ear for languages*.

11 People who are *high-flyers* usually work in the airline industry.

12 Losing the job he enjoyed was *a huge burden off his shoulders*.

13 The beautiful young princess was *a sight for sore eyes*.

14 If you are *on the dole*, you are out of work.

15 The teacher was so experienced that Ken couldn't *pull the wool over her eyes* when he said the dog had eaten his homework.

16 Daniel was *walking on air* when he got the job of his dreams.